Foundation for Your Success

The Power of Competence

Sculpting the Best Version of Yourself

The Power of Competence

Sculpting the Best Version of Yourself

By **Sirshree** Tejparkhi

Tejgyan Global Foundation is a charitable organization
with its headquarters in Pune, India.

ISBN : 978-93-47087-12-7

Published by WOW Publishings Pvt. Ltd., India

First edition published in November 2025

Printed and bound by Parksons Graphics Pvt. Ltd.

This book is based on the Hindi book titled,
Safaltaa ki Buniyaad - Kaabiliyat by **Sirshree** Tejparkhi

To all teachers and mentors
who recognize others' capabilities
and empower them to actualize their potential.

Content

Preface

Competence Precedes Success

A beehive swayed gently on a large branch of a tree in the garden, surrounded by a swarm of buzzing bees.

Twelve-year-old Rohit stood gazing at the distant tree. His grandfather, who was standing beside him, glanced at Rohit and followed his gaze. He thoughtfully said, "Everyone knows about honey, but seldom do people think of the bees' relentless dedication and arduous labor to create it."

"Grandpa," Rohit asked, his curiosity evident, "How do these little bees create such a big beehive? How much honey does a single bee make?"

Grandpa began marveling, "The bees may be small. In their entire lifespan, each bee makes a mere one-twelfth of a spoonful of honey. However, it's not just a single bee building its hive; thousands work together in perfect synergy, driven by instinct and the predominant need of the colony. Their remarkable coordination involves making thousands of trips to flowers to gather nectar, which collectively adds up to thousands of kilometers of flying. Indeed, their beehives are big testaments to their incredibly intricate teamwork, collective intelligence, persistence, perseverance, resilience, and hard work. You will be mesmerized by their capabilities and inspired to develop similar qualities in yourself. There is a great deal to learn from them."

"Grandpa, I am eager to understand how they work together," Rohit exclaimed.

Grandpa happily explained, "A honeybee colony is a highly organized society with a clear division of labor among three distinct types of bees—the queen bee, the male bee, and the worker bee—each with unique roles and traits. The queen bee is the undisputed leader of the hive. She is typically the largest bee and the only fertile female in the colony. The queen bee and male bee are responsible for reproduction. The queen bee lays eggs. The worker bees, constituting most of the hive's population, are the true workforce of the colony. They perform every task necessary for the hive's survival and prosperity. They fly out and gather nectar from flowers to make honey. The harmonious interaction between these three types of bees, each fulfilling their duties, ensures the efficiency, growth, and survival of the entire honeybee colony."

Grandpa continued, "From the life of honeybees, we learn that the secret behind achieving proficiency and success lies in consistent hard work, organized teamwork, and unwavering self-belief. No matter how small our effort may be, when we sincerely work with full dedication and commitment, we see a remarkable transformation over time."

Though small, Rohit was mature and intelligent for his age. After intently listening to Grandpa, he declared with a newfound resolve, "Grandpa, henceforth, I will also fully focus on my studies. I will form a study group with my friends, and we will work together to finish our assignments."

If we draw inspiration from the life of bees, we can learn a lot from their hard work and qualities. Like bees, when small, consistent effort is channeled in the right direction, we can also hone our innate capabilities and become truly competent.

You must have noticed that, typically, any important task is entrusted only to someone considered capable of managing it. The bigger the task, the more responsibilities or risks it involves, so a more qualified and competent individual is chosen for it.

For instance, to find relief from your illness, you would surely consult a doctor who specializes in treating it. Similarly, when choosing a sports team, only those who have mastered the game are selected.

In fact, we are all born with some inherent talents that are blessings bestowed upon us by nature. However, for other skills, we need to build our capabilities and nurture qualities aligned with our goals.

For instance, a child's conception is a blessing, but it requires parents to be able to nurture that child and instill the right values in them. When the child wants to play outside, they need to be able to walk on their own first. Later on, they need to develop their capability at each stage of life, whether attending school or college, earning a livelihood, or navigating life's experiences.

Just as a strong foundation is laid to ensure a building stands tall and firm for years, you need to build a solid foundation to succeed in any field or accomplish something significant. To achieve this, you need to become competent in that area. When you learn to make the most of even the smallest opportunities that life offers, you enhance your capabilities.

Life offers us many opportunities to take on new tasks. By recognizing and using them wisely, we can enhance our capabilities. In essence, a competent person regards every task as an opportunity for learning and growth.

Otherwise, people often say, "I only have to do everything myself. I have to take care of all my family members, tolerate such difficult neighbors, handle all sorts of tasks at work, toil day and night, manage my health," and so on. They keep grumbling, "I only have to do this and that"—that becomes their way of speaking. But the one who wants to work on their competence and realize their potential says, "I'm getting an opportunity to do this; this is becoming instrumental for unlocking my possibilities."

Do you take advantage of the opportunities that come your way in life, or do you let them slip by? You possess many hidden qualities. To unlock your full potential, you need to learn to make the most of the opportunities life offers. This will help reveal your hidden abilities, elevate your competence to the next level, and lay the foundation for success and self-confidence.

Getting the right guidance is essential to enhancing competence, and this book will serve as a true mentor. Besides outlining different ways to improve competence, it also contains engaging stories that impart 12 key qualities. The goal is for you to become competent first and then achieve success, because competence precedes success.

Now, close your eyes for a few moments and pray: "I will embrace all the qualities given in this book, so that they contribute to developing myself, my family, my community, and society at large, thereby helping everyone reach the pinnacle of success."

So, like Rohit, are you ready to develop your physical and mental competence? Are you willing to put in the effort by embracing the principle: **Competence precedes success?**

If your answer is "Yes," you have already won half the battle. And if your answer is "No," read the entire book and ask yourself this question again.

Wishing you all the best!

PART 1

BE WORTHY OF BECOMING COMPETENT

1

What is Competence

"Who'll be the competent one chosen for this opportunity?" The question hung in the air as the office meeting buzzed with anticipation. Everyone was eager to hear the announcement, but selecting the right person proved to be challenging. The competition was fierce, yet only one individual would be chosen.

As usual, the meeting commenced at 10:00 a.m. With five shortlisted candidates in focus, the team began its analysis. Discussion ensued regarding their competence and suitability. All were competent in their own way, but since only one could be selected, the question arose: What criteria should be applied in the selection process? How could they identify the most capable candidate?

Some equated competence with having specific skills and professional acumen, while others argued that certain traits and qualities were the true measure of competence. Everyone tried to define the criteria for competence in their own way, as they perceived it differently. Ultimately, it became challenging to define competence in a single, concise manner.

Pause for a moment and reflect: What does competence truly mean to you? If you had to select someone for an important project, who would you consider competent?

1. One who has technical proficiency or project management skills but lacks other essential qualities.
2. One who possesses many qualities such as commitment, dedication, and punctuality, but lacks the necessary work-related knowledge.
3. One who has many years of experience in the field but lacks other essential skills and qualities.
4. Or, one who has a blend of some qualities and experience, but most importantly, they have the passion and perseverance to get the task completed. People have faith that if a task is entrusted to them, they will surely complete it and deliver the best result.

Now, let's understand what true competence is. We are not born with inherent competence. While we possess certain innate qualities, like patience, honesty, kindness, and compassion, we also need to develop other qualities, like communication, creativity, confidence, and integrity, to lead a principled life. All these qualities strengthen our foundation. When we nurture these qualities, we become truly competent.

A competent person can confidently adapt to any situation and, with a passion for learning and perseverance, complete tasks effectively. They can prove their worth in any field they get an opportunity in. When others also believe in their abilities, they are regarded as competent.

True competence is not measured solely by external awards or achievements. It is not just about winning. Someone who emerges as the winner in a competition is undoubtedly competent, but so are those who strive and participate, regardless of their final rankings. Competence is not dependent on achieving a specific outcome or holding a particular position; it is about the pursuit—the effort, determination, and commitment to persevere.

Let's understand this with an example.

Aditya was a young employee at a large multinational company. He was technically proficient and completed every project ahead of schedule, with flawless precision. Everyone admired his abilities. However, despite his hard work, he was not getting promoted or assigned to bigger projects.

One day, the company launched a major project and included Aditya as part of the team. However, Kavya, a senior manager known for her extensive experience and strategic vision, was asked to lead the project.

Aditya diligently completed his work and submitted it to Kavya well ahead of schedule. However, upon reviewing his work, Kavya offered him some feedback, "Aditya, you've done your work well. However, you've only focused on the technical aspects. You also need to consider the client's requirements, understand market trends, and present everything effectively."

At first, Aditya was disheartened to hear this, but he embraced it as a learning opportunity. While working with Kavya, he observed how skillfully she understood the client's requirements, analyzed market data, and leveraged her expertise to advance the project to the next level.

Gradually, Aditya began learning these new skills. He no longer focused merely on completing tasks on time, but also meticulously worked on every small detail with great depth and precision. He learned to communicate with clients and started to view the project from a holistic perspective.

A year later, when the company undertook another major project, Aditya was chosen to lead the team. Leveraging both his inherent abilities and newly acquired skills, he completed the project with excellence.

When we approach any task with skill and the right mindset, it enhances our capability and brings true success. However, when we fail in any area, we tend to see ourselves as incapable. But no one is inherently incapable; everyone has untapped potential. We need to strive to unlock that hidden potential through persistent effort.

Life presents numerous opportunities to refine our qualities, hone our skills, and improve our efficiency. However, trapped in a cycle of self-doubt, we fail to seize these possibilities and continue to perceive ourselves as incapable.

It is like owning a premium edition of a book signed by a renowned author, carefully kept in the bookshelf. The owner could have benefitted by reading it, but instead, they boast about having the signed copy. They never take it out. Eventually, the book just wears away in the bookshelf. What would you advise them?

Of course, you would advise them to take it out and read it. Similarly, we must actively develop and practice our skills, capabilities, and qualities, and sharpen them through the tasks we undertake to unleash our full potential.

Competence is not acquired in a day. Just as people work tirelessly day and night to build wealth, we must also consistently work to develop competence. Although we may not see the results immediately, they will become apparent over time. Thus, competence is not just an inherent talent but a quality nurtured through hard work, dedication, and unwavering resolve.

Now, the choice is yours: Do you want to continue living the way you have been? Or are you prepared to put in the effort needed to enhance your competence? Are you ready to embark on the journey to becoming competent right away with this book?

2

Competence - a Goal

After completing his medical studies, Amar opened his clinic and began his practice. Initially, while treating patients, he felt the need to stay up to date on the latest research, treatments, and technologies. However, he shirked away from doing it, thinking, "Let it be. I'm earning enough for a living." He continued treating patients solely with his existing knowledge, but they did not achieve the expected results.

A few days later, the patients began visiting more competent doctors and were cured of their illnesses. They started spreading the word about Amar's ineffectiveness, discouraging others from consulting him. Gradually, this led to a significant decline in the patients visiting him.

Amar was initially baffled by the sudden drop in the patients' turnout at his clinic. However, he gradually realized that his professional stagnation stemmed from his lethargy and lack of competence. Acknowledging this hard truth, he made the difficult decision to close his clinic and take a job as an assistant doctor at a hospital. This proved to be a turning point in his career.

At the hospital, Amar underwent a profound transformation. As an assistant, he acquired hands-on medical skills by performing a wide range of procedures under the supervision of his seniors. The structured environment and mentorship from seniors forced him to overcome his laziness and develop a strong work ethic. His work accountability led him to learn new treatment modalities and stay current with the latest research. He also enrolled in and acquired professional certification in his niche. He gained thorough experience in dealing with many patients from diverse backgrounds. Beyond just seeing patients as a source of income, a deep sense of compassion and a genuine desire to serve them gradually grew within him. Within a few years, through his dedicated hard work, unwavering commitment, continuous skill development, and patient care, he became a competent practitioner.

Amar's story highlights the significance of competence. Initially, when he began his medical practice at his clinic, he did not update himself with the latest research and treatment modalities to meet his professional demands. Hence, people stopped visiting him. However, after updating his skills and knowledge by working at the hospital, he became a competent doctor. Thus, practical experience with updated skills is essential for becoming competent.

Imagine someone who has read many books on driving but is driving for the first time. Would you travel in a car driven by that person?

You will surely agree that anyone can acquire the theoretical knowledge of driving and even explain every step or memorize all the rules by attending courses or reading handbooks. However, merely gaining knowledge does not make one capable of applying it effectively. True competence demands far more. For that, they need to be trained by a qualified instructor first and then practice driving for some time. Only after successfully driving several times can they become competent enough to transport others safely.

Pause for a moment and reflect: How do you envision your life? What is your ultimate goal? Do you just aim to earn money and live an easy life? Do you dream of winning a lottery and having everything taken care of while you relax at home? Or do you aspire to become proficient and highly capable in everything you do?

True competence gives you a distinct edge. Hence, setting the goal of developing competence is of utmost importance.

An average person often neglects developing their capabilities; as a result, they lead a stressful life. Conversely, those who invest their time and effort in enhancing their capabilities find all their tasks completed smoothly and efficiently, in a free-flow manner, on time. Regardless of the adverse situations they face in any area of their life, they skillfully navigate them with confidence and composure. The positive impact of their developed capabilities resonates not only in their own lives but also in those around them.

Now, the decision is yours: whether to pursue wealth or capability, a position or true ability, a mere passing grade or genuine competence.

People often prioritize accumulating wealth over developing their competence. This trend extends to children who study not to develop genuine competence, but to pass exams and achieve high scores. Their teachers and parents often push them to strive for top ranks and instill a sense of competition in them. Instead, they should be taught, "Don't study merely to pass or secure grades. Study honestly to develop your competence." The Bollywood film "3 Idiots" so aptly demonstrates, "Study to become capable, not just to pass the exams." If you are capable, success will naturally follow, bringing with it wealth, desired positions, and good grades.

As you cultivate your capability, you acquire the underlying skills and knowledge, becoming proficient in handling tasks and situations effectively. When you consistently perform well, you develop competence, and success inevitably follows. When you succeed, it reinforces your skills and boosts your confidence. It also opens doors to new opportunities and responsibilities that further promote your growth and expand your overall capability. Thus, success, in turn, further enhances your capability, setting in motion a powerful cycle of growth. The diagram below illustrates this cycle.

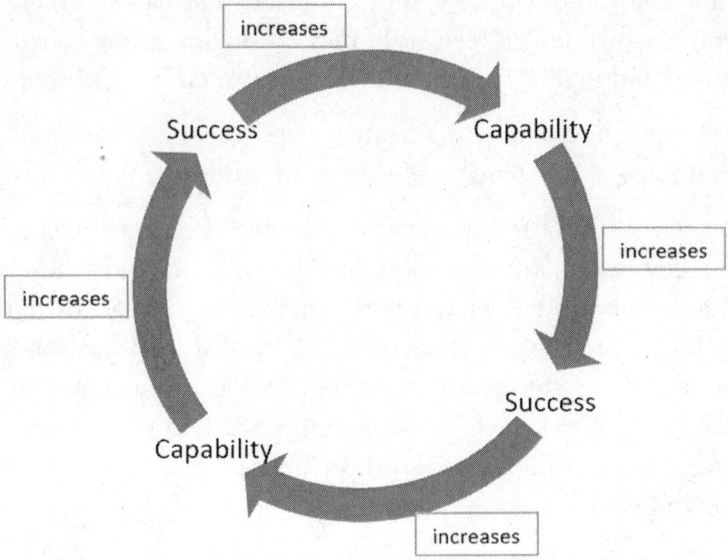

Let's understand the scientific reason behind honing our capabilities. Just as our body needs physical exercise to stay healthy, our brain also needs exercise for our cognitive well-being. We lift weights to strengthen our muscles; similarly, our brain's neural pathways are exercised when we work on improving the core components of our intelligence, such as memory, processing speed, attention and focus, reasoning, and problem-solving.

Thus, the more we challenge our brain and learn new things, the healthier our existing neurons become. Additionally, new neurons are formed, and new neural pathways are created. This ongoing activity keeps our brain active, which boosts its capacity and health, and prevents cognitive decline. Hence, we must regularly exercise our brain with diverse and stimulating activities.

Our brain has over 80 billion neurons to give us strength and make us capable, but we utilize only a tiny fraction of them. Those who engage in solving new puzzles, playing chess, and completing crossword puzzles from an early age essentially exercise their brain and stay active. These practices help them become more capable.

Besides these activities, challenge yourself regularly to keep your brain active. For example, to cultivate a new habit, you can challenge yourself, "I will consistently work on this for X number of days." If you miss a day, restart the challenge from scratch. If you complete it successfully, raise the bar by extending the duration or setting a new, more ambitious goal. You might also take on a challenge to meditate for a set number of days, as meditation is a scientifically proven practice for effectively stimulating neurogenesis.

While most of us know about the proper dietary and supplement needs of our body, we often overlook the specific needs of our brain. Investing in our brain's development is the highway to enhancing our capability. Following the "Use it or lose it" principle, if we do not effectively use our brain, we risk losing our ability to learn new things and adapt. Therefore, we must cultivate the habit of continuously learning new things.

Remember, capability is a fundamental requirement for excellence in any field—be it doctors, carpenters, drivers, pilots, fashion designers, athletes, scientists, or homemakers. Those who consistently strive to improve their capabilities and prioritize excellence not only achieve success but also cultivate the ability to sustain it over time.

3

Recognize Opportunities to Develop Competence

Long ago, a king named Amarshakti ruled the kingdom of Mahilaropyam in southern India. He was a master of science, politics, and ethics, and was well-loved by his subjects. He had three sons who, unfortunately, were lazy and dull; they lacked the wisdom and intellect required for leadership. The king, who cared for the well-being of his subjects, was worried about what would happen after him. How would the incompetent princes possibly govern the kingdom?

Even for driving a car, a skilled and competent driver is required; otherwise, people's lives can be at risk. In this case, ruling a kingdom demanded an even greater degree of wisdom and competence. The king was well aware of this and was anxious to develop the essential competence in his sons.

One day, he summoned his key ministers and shared his concerns. The ministers advised, "The princes should learn economics, ethics, law, and religion. However, mastering these subjects would require at least twelve years."

"Twelve years!" the king lamented. "What will be the state of the kingdom by then? Not sure whether I will be there. But what is the guarantee that they will learn? My concerns persist."

Then, Sumati, the most capable among the ministers, proposed, "Instead of burdening the princes with exhaustive knowledge, let us impart only the essence of the knowledge that will help them become virtuous kings, just as a swan discerns water, consuming only the milk."

"That sounds both practical and wise," the king conceded. "But how do we go about this, and who is capable of doing it?"

Sumati replied, "I know of a teacher named Pandit Vishnu Sharma. He possesses profound knowledge of all the scriptures and is highly regarded among his students for his unique teaching style. If you permit, I can call him to the royal court. If he agrees to teach the princes, you can be free of your worries."

The king agreed, and Pandit Vishnu Sharma was summoned. After listening intently, he said, "Your Majesty, I would like to see the princes first and observe them closely."

The king granted permission and offered him a generous reward: "O wise master, if you succeed in this great endeavor, I'll reward you with a hundred villages."

Pandit Vishnu Sharma watched the children discreetly from a distance. He observed their activities all day long—their behavior, arguments, mischief, and destructive tendencies. He understood that the three princes also possessed some capabilities.

Pandit Vishnu Sharma returned to the king and declared, "Your Majesty, I'll impart knowledge to your sons. I will prepare them within six months."

Astonished and overjoyed, the king exclaimed, "O wise master, if the results are achieved so fast, you can ask for whatever you wish."

Pandit Vishnu Sharma calmly replied, "Your Majesty, I desire nothing, not even the hundred villages. I see this as an opportunity to enhance both my competence and theirs."

Not only did Pandit Vishnu Sharma accept the herculean task as an opportunity, but he also embraced it as a challenge for himself and declared, "Your Majesty, if I fail to achieve this within six months, you may sentence me to death."

Impressed by his resolve, the king felt a great burden lifted from his heart. That night, he slept soundly and began managing his kingdom's affairs with renewed peace of mind.

Pandit Vishnu Sharma took the princes along but realized that the traditional teaching method would not work with them. Recognizing their short attention spans, he decided to harness the power of storytelling. He crafted a series of captivating fables in which animals spoke like humans, conveying key lessons through the storylines.

The princes listened with rapt attention. As the stories unfolded, they began to grasp practical wisdom and learned how to navigate real-life situations. Gradually, their understanding deepened.

Thus, through Pandit Vishnu Sharma's creative and insightful method, King Amarshakti succeeded in developing the competence his sons needed to govern the kingdom.

You may wonder, "How did Pandit Vishnu Sharma possess such unwavering confidence to teach the princes?" Let's understand it.

If we wish to accomplish something grand and worthwhile in life, we need to develop the necessary skills and competence. Life presents us with numerous opportunities to engage in new activities. When we recognize these opportunities, however insignificant they may appear, and seize and leverage them for our growth, it enhances our competence. This is the very foundation of success and confidence.

In this case, Pandit Vishnu Sharma faced the herculean task of imparting the essence of knowledge to the unwise princes, of all people, and that too in such a short time. It was a seemingly impossible task! However, he took it as an opportunity, believing in his competence and aiming to elevate it to the next level. He was not driven by the reward of a hundred villages, but what truly mattered to him was the satisfaction of successfully completing the task. As his competence developed further, every story went on to become a part of the famous collection, "Tales from the Panchatantra." This served as a medium through which wisdom reached people around the world.

Pause for a moment and reflect: Like Pandit Vishnu Sharma, do we genuinely seize and leverage the opportunities that come our way in life, or do we just let them slip away?

If we also want to unlock the hidden qualities within us and fully realize our potential, we must learn to take advantage of the opportunities that life offers.

You may have often heard people lamenting: "I've to do everything for the family. I've to tolerate the neighbors. I've to accomplish so many activities in the job. I've to look after the children. I've to deal with so many problems in society. I've to perform these daily chores and toil hard day and night. I've to look after my health, and so on." The bottom line is they always think, "I have to do everything." But those who want to develop their competence say, "I've got the opportunity to do this work. It will help unlock the possibilities within me."

In fact, the human body holds immense potential and vast reserves of strength. But do we actively tap into these resources? Do we strive to unleash our highest possibilities?

Often, we let opportunities slip away by making excuses such as "I can't do this work," "I have never worked on this before," "I have no time for this," or "I lack the required skill." If we repeatedly dismiss opportunities and keep doing the same old tasks, how can we develop new qualities, talents, or capabilities?

If you wish to enhance your competence, you must take advantage of the small opportunities that life presents daily. For instance, if you are an employee and there is an event at your workplace, seize the chance to host the program or organize food for everyone. If you are a homemaker, you can participate in your child's school project. If you are a student, you can deliver a speech on stage or participate in sports activities. All these opportunities help to unveil your inherent capabilities.

Therefore, to realize your full potential, consider every task as an opportunity for growth. This will uncover your hidden competence, scale your talents and abilities to new heights, and lay the foundation for your lasting success and confidence.

4

The Science of Deliberate Practice

Imagine you are given a crazy ball that defies all logic with its unpredictable bounces. As it changes direction randomly with every bounce, you cannot anticipate its path.

Your challenge is to catch it. The ball bounces erratically, rebounding off walls and the furniture around, slipping past your grasp every time. However hard you try, despite repeated attempts, you fail to catch it.

What would you do to succeed? Yes, you guessed it right! You have to become competent enough before trying to catch the crazy ball. First, study the ball's behavior, its erratic bouncing patterns, how long it stays in the air, and so on. Then, practice catching the ball consistently. After investing your valuable time in this practice, attentively observe and analyze each move so you can discern the subtle variations of each of its bounces.

Once you become an expert with the ball, try bouncing it on different surfaces, like a soft bed, a wooden table, a plush carpet, smooth tiles, rough ground, and even a perfectly flat floor. When you become competent in bouncing the crazy ball on any surface, under any condition, you will have achieved proficiency in the game. With this newfound mastery and confidence, you can declare, "Now, I can play on any surface; I'm ready."

Our life is also like a crazy ball. It has its ups and downs. Sometimes, life can be stable, while at other times, it can be disrupted by sudden, unforeseen, unpredictable events. Some people constantly face various challenges in their lives, such as physical health issues, strained relationships at home and at work, financial hardships, or unexpected life changes. To effectively navigate these challenges, you will need to enhance your capability. Only then can you confidently say, "Come what may, I'm ready to live life to the fullest."

For this, you will need to practice consistently in every facet of your life. The more diligently you practice, the more proficient you become. For instance, legendary cricketer Sachin Tendulkar has not achieved his unparalleled mastery in the sport due to a few days' practice. It was the result of his years of unwavering dedication and relentless hard work in pursuit of perfection. The countless hours he spent honing his skills are a testament to his enduring patience and profound expertise.

Remember, the power of practice lies in repetition—performing a task over and over again. When we repeatedly perform a task, our brain and body gradually develop proficiency in it.

Let's understand it with the example of riding a bicycle. When one learns to ride a bicycle for the first time, their attention is divided between pedaling, steering the handlebars, and maintaining the elusive balance of the bicycle. However, as they practice daily, they gradually become proficient. This demonstrates the power of consistent repetition.

Malcolm Gladwell, the Canadian journalist, author, and public speaker has discussed the powerful "10,000-hour rule" in his book "Outliers." He states that "The key to achieving true expertise in any skill is simply a matter of practicing, albeit in the correct way, for at least 10,000 hours. This isn't just about doing; it's about practicing the right way, with intensity and focus."

Many of the world's top musicians, athletes, writers, and scientists have achieved excellence in their fields by adopting this principle, either consciously or instinctively. This principle states that talent alone is not enough; true success comes from relentless effort, consistent and dedicated practice, and unwavering commitment.

There are examples of many people who have put in 10,000 hours of deliberate practice in various fields. For instance, public speakers like Tony Robbins and Oprah Winfrey spent more than 10,000 hours perfecting their skills to achieve mastery. Writers like J. K. Rowling and Stephen King have invested more than 10,000 hours in their niche to gain expertise.

Famous Indian translator Sudhir Dixit has dedicated over 10,000 hours to mastering the art of translation. He has translated many international bestsellers, including the Harry Potter series, into Hindi. His exceptional skill allows him to translate an entire book in just three to four days. Additionally, he is currently writing his own books. This shows his strong commitment to writing and deep expertise, both developed through relentless practice and steadfast dedication.

Famous author J.K. Rowling's dedicated hours to writing led to the creation of a literary phenomenon. She spent years writing and rewriting with perseverance, often while facing hardships. She wrote in cafes while raising her daughter alone and living on welfare. Harry Potter, reportedly written over five years, was rejected by 12 publishers before Bloomsbury took a chance. She became one of the best-selling authors in history—clearly the result of not just talent, but also countless hours of crafting story, character, and style.

You can see how one can achieve expertise with sustained effort and practice. Hence, instead of merely focusing on earning academic qualifications, focus on becoming competent and investing 10,000 hours —a substantial, dedicated time commitment. If you cannot dedicate that much time, at least give sufficient time to execute your tasks with precision and finesse consistently within the given time. The more repeatedly you accomplish your tasks, the more capable you become, and this mastery leads to record-breaking achievements.

"Behind every great achievement are years of hard work." If you can dedicate 10,000 hours in the right way, success will surely follow you. However, even after achieving success, consistent practice is essential to sustain it.

Consider accomplished artists; no matter how successful they become, they never give up their practice. Throughout history, all accomplished artists have maintained an unwavering dedication to practice, irrespective of their level of achievement. Singers practice daily to refine and preserve their vocal prowess. A renowned singer once remarked, "If I miss a day of practice, I notice the difference in my voice. If, for some reason, I am unable to practice for two days, my accompanists notice it. But if I neglect my practice for four or more days, even my audience can feel the difference."

Similarly, our goal is not to become capable only once, but to continually improve that capability through daily or weekly practice as needed. The greater the goal, the more ability and practice are required. Further, the level of skill and practice depends on the complexity of the task.

If someone wants to ride a tricycle, less skill and practice will suffice. If they are going to ride a bicycle, they need a bit more ability and significantly more practice. If they want to ride a scooter or a bike, they will need to shift gears—so they will need to improve their skills and practice. If they are going to drive a car, fly a helicopter, or launch a rocket, they will need that level of capability and intensive practice. For launching a rocket, they will need many years of intensive training and practice. Otherwise, they will not even be permitted to go near a rocket, let alone launch it. The same applies to becoming a pilot; they must undergo years of rigorous training and practice before gaining the necessary skills, and only then are they allowed in the cockpit.

Pause for a moment and reflect: If mastering these skills demands such significant effort and unwavering dedication, how much more profound a level of competence is required to navigate the intricate tapestry of life itself?

Often, people spend a lot of time and energy developing various professional skills but neglect cultivating the fundamental competencies necessary for a fulfilling and meaningful life. Therefore, it is crucial to prioritize developing the skills needed to live with finesse, purpose, and effectiveness.

Once you gain mastery in any field or skill through continuous practice, use that as a springboard to elevate to the next level. Just as in academics, after completing one grade, you can progress to the next. Similarly, when you consistently work on your qualities and hone them, they become part of your life. Then, to elevate to the next level and unlock your hidden potential, you need to take on some challenging or different activities that boost your qualities. The more you freely express your qualities, the easier it becomes to transition smoothly to the next level of growth.

Remember, mere qualifications on paper are not enough; your capability matters much more. The competence that stems from experience and the expertise gained through practice are more important. Therefore, develop the ability to engage in continuous learning and growth. It is this enduring commitment that truly unlocks your potential.

5

Initial Steps to Unleash Your Competence

Everything was peaceful and well-ordered in Sharada's life. Her life revolved around household chores, caring for her in-laws, and living a contented life with her husband, Kamal. But one evening, when Kamal took her to an office party, her life took an unexpected turn that she had never imagined. Her hidden passion, a smoldering fire that had been suppressed for years, was unexpectedly rekindled at the party.

That evening, Sharada was dressed in an elegant traditional attire. As she entered the hall with a radiant smile and a sparkle in her eyes, her eyes fell upon a harmonium placed on a table in the corner. The sight of it instantly transported her back to her childhood days.

Sharada's childhood was spent in a music-loving environment. Music held a special place in her home, and this art virtually became an integral part of her life. Every morning, her mother would wake up and sing devotional hymns. From a young age, Sharada would accompany her, listening to her hymns and humming along.

Recognizing her budding talent, Sharada's father encouraged her to hone her skills. To pursue formal training, he enrolled her with a skilled classical music teacher. She grew so fond of music that she began dedicating all her free time to practicing and learning it. Gradually, her voice gained a remarkable sweetness and a rich, profound depth.

Everyone in her family appreciated and encouraged her talent, and she resolved to make singing a lifelong passion. However, as time passed, her responsibilities multiplied, and her connection to music began to wane. After her marriage, she seemed to have forgotten singing altogether. Her elderly in-laws required extra care, so she prioritized their well-being and dedicated her time to them. As she balanced all her responsibilities, her cherished childhood passion faded into the background.

The party vibe was vibrant and festive. Colorful lights illuminated the hall, creating a joyous atmosphere throughout. A gentle, fragrant breeze drifted through the air. The band's live music on stage made the atmosphere even more energetic and lively.

Unexpectedly, Kamal's boss invited everyone to sing. Some people enthusiastically participated. Then, it was Sharada's turn. She had not had a chance to sing in years. A mix of excitement and nervousness washed over her. Unable to decline the invitation, she made her way to the stage.

As she held the microphone, her heart raced, but soon a unique sense of calm settled over her. The moment she began to sing, the entire hall fell utterly silent. Her voice, imbued with a rare, long-lost sweetness and soulful depth, captivated everyone. As she finished, a wave of thunderous applause erupted in the hall. Respect and admiration were evident on every face.

Kamal watched her with pride. A new hope gleamed in his eyes as he fully realized her hidden talent. The people at the party showered her with praise. Many even suggested that she should pursue a professional singing career. But Sharada gently laughed and dismissed these suggestions. She knew that music was her first love, but she felt bound by her duties, believing there was no room for it in her life.

Yet, a strange restlessness stirred deep within her. She tried to reassure herself that it was merely fleeting excitement, but a small spark had ignited deep within, in a corner of her heart. Sleep eluded her that night as questions swirled in her mind: "Can I rekindle that passion once again? Can I dare to fulfill my dream? Can I revive that love that had been buried for so long?" Finally, taking a few deep breaths and pushing the thoughts aside, she drifted into sleep.

The next morning, over tea, Kamal said, "Sharada, you have a unique talent. The sweetness in your voice is a rare gift that not everyone possesses. If you truly want to pursue it, I'm with you. We can work on this together. Perhaps this is the right time to make your dreams a reality."

His words seemed like an indication from nature. Sharada decided to embrace her reawakened passion.

Like Sharada, many people have latent qualities, talent, and skills. However, for various reasons, they are unable to use them, and these qualities often remain dormant and suppressed. With a little conscious effort and practice, they can nurture these qualities and gradually enhance their competence to accomplish significant feats. In doing so, they can also showcase their talent and competence to the world.

The following steps can help enhance competence.

1. Seek opportunities, create needs

Many people have the opportunity to prove their competence by enhancing their inner qualities when such a need arises in their lives, driven by certain situations and challenges. To earn a livelihood, they take on jobs or start businesses, through which they can enhance their competence. However, some people do not feel this need, so they do not make any such effort and neglect developing their innate talent. Yet, one should not strive only for earning money; they can work to do something new to bring out their qualities and enhance their competence.

Often, people bring out their true capabilities when faced with challenging situations or urgent needs. For instance, an older woman with a talent for running fast participated in a marathon to raise money for her husband's medical treatment. She won the prize money and showcased her unique talent to the world.

Similarly, in the 17th century, during the reign of the Maratha King Shivaji Maharaj, a milkmaid named Hirkani was trapped inside Raigad Fort after the gates were closed. She displayed remarkable courage and resourcefulness when she dared to climb down a steep cliff in the dead of night to return to her infant son.

Air hostess Neerja Bhanot became a symbol of bravery to the world when she courageously protected the lives of passengers on a hijacked plane through her exceptional courage and quick thinking.

These are just a few examples of people who demonstrated their exceptional abilities to the world. There are countless others who showcased their capabilities when faced with urgent needs or challenging circumstances.

Pause for a moment and reflect: Should we wait for such situations to arise to bring out and enhance our capabilities? Or should we proactively unleash our hidden talent, express it, and unlock new possibilities for ourselves?

The human body holds immense potential. We need to actively work to unlock some of these possibilities. We must create opportunities and situations ourselves that allow our latent qualities to surface. If we look within, we will find that some of our qualities have become dormant because we have not used them for a long time. However, if we allow these qualities to blossom, they can enhance our competence.

For instance, if you have a talent for teaching or possess artistic or technical skills, you can teach them to the children in your neighborhood, or on online platforms. If you excelled at a particular sport in your childhood but could not pursue it due to your career demands, you can coach kids in the evenings. You will feel satisfied by doing this. Even if you do not need to earn money using these talent, you can create opportunities to fulfill your passion, which will, in turn, enhance your competence.

2. Fuel your desires

Some people aspire to do something but lack the confidence to act. They either wait perpetually for the perfect moment or resign themselves to blaming fate. Meanwhile, others are held back by lethargy and never feel ready to act.

To overcome this, you need to empower your desires and dreams to accomplish something and infuse them with life. Do not wait for someone else to motivate you; you must motivate yourself.

Visualize that your dreams and desires are already fulfilled. Close your eyes and envision the joy you would feel after fulfilling your dreams and desires, expressing your talents, and enhancing your competence. This will strengthen your resolve to fulfill your desires and help you boost your competence.

A burning desire compels us to find the time to pursue it. You, too, can seek out or create opportunities in your life, generate the need, and strengthen your desire to enhance your competence.

Remember, enhancing your competence has no age limit or time constraints. If you are passionate about learning, you can learn any skill at any age or under any circumstances. In today's rapidly evolving world, everyone yearns to progress and advance. But this is possible only when they become competent enough to do so.

6

Navigate Life's Challenges

Anuja was a bright and hardworking student. After completing high school, she moved to another city to pursue her dream of studying engineering. She rented an apartment with some of her classmates and began her studies with complete dedication. Initially, her friends were equally committed, but with no one to keep them in check, their attention soon drifted to socializing and having fun.

Seeing her friends enjoying themselves, Anuja began to think, "They're having so much fun, and I'm just studying all the time." She confided in her mother about it. Her mother advised her, "Anuja, stay away from all this for now. This is just a passing phase. Just as your unwavering effort in your 10th and 12th grades got you into engineering, your hard work now will pave the way to a successful career and a better life in the future."

Anuja agreed with her mother's advice and refocused on her studies. Soon, the first-year examinations were over, and the results were out. While her friends failed in three or four subjects, Anuja scored well in all except Mathematics. She failed in Mathematics by just two points. She was totally disheartened.

She began to think, "Now, this 'Fail' remark will forever damage my biodata. Even if I pass this subject next year, it won't matter. If there is a 'Fail' remark, companies will outrightly reject me. I won't even get a chance to appear for the written tests or interviews. Then, how will I be able to show my capability and prove myself? I'll face a lot of trouble finding a job. Maybe I should just quit engineering."

During her vacation, when she returned home, she was so sad that she stayed apart from others. She didn't talk to anyone or go out anywhere. To lift her spirits, her mother suggested she meet up with her old friends. She met Priya, one of her closest friends, and confided all her doubts and fears to her.

Priya tried to make her understand and reminded her, "You have dreamed of becoming an engineer since childhood. And now that your dream is coming true, why are you getting stuck on such a small thing and holding yourself back? Do you think you can study with the same confidence in any other field and be happy? Although you have failed in a subject this year, you have scored well in the other subjects. If you continue your studies with full dedication and hard work, you will surely perform well in the future and achieve higher grades. There could be some companies that value competence over grades."

Priya's encouraging words lifted her spirits and motivated her, as she hadn't thought this way before. She had seen a minor academic setback as a complete failure and felt unworthy. She was about to give up on her promising, bright future, treating a small obstacle as an insurmountable barrier.

Today, a decade later, she was on her way to meet Priya. All those formative moments played out like scenes from a cherished, nostalgic movie. She gently smiled to herself as she recalled her youthful, naïve behavior. A wave of profound gratitude washed over her for her mother and Priya, who had guided her through both joy and sorrow. It had paved the way for her present success. She was now working in a senior position at a Fortune 100 company and living a contented married life with her family.

Meanwhile, her former classmates, who were enjoying themselves at the time, thought, "No one is stopping us, so why shouldn't we hang out, have fun, and enjoy ourselves? Studies will always be there." However, they had to pay a heavy price for getting caught in that small bit of happiness. As they failed in more than three subjects, they couldn't get admission to the next year and had to repeat the same year. Additionally, their habit of unchecked freedom and immediate gratification led them to prioritize fleeting pleasures over discipline. As a result, they lost focus on their studies and barely managed to pass. Though they eventually earned their engineering degrees, they had to settle for mediocre jobs with lower salaries than their peers. Their inclination toward extravagance and indulgence in comfort and convenience left them constantly short of money, leading to conflicts in their families and relationships.

You may have observed how an ant shows relentless perseverance when it encounters an obstacle like a stone or a piece of wood. It neither gives up nor retreats but rather navigates around it or climbs over it. Similarly, those who strive to enhance their competence also face such challenges. They sometimes feel incapable of overcoming or solving these problems and abandon their pursuits prematurely. However, if they draw inspiration from ants and continually seek solutions to their problems, they will soon enhance their abilities and start walking on the path to success.

Let's explore the precautions needed to hone our skills and enhance our competence.

1. Overcome the lack of discipline

Just like a daydreamer, people often build elaborate castles of success in the air, only to crumble when it is time to act, and the undisciplined mind begins to make excuses that hinder progress. For example, an above-average student resolved to excel in his master's program and envision a bright career. To achieve this, he needed to study each subject consistently and diligently throughout the academic year.

However, he was accustomed to studying only for the last two months. As a result, he found studying for hours at the beginning of the year boring, and, due to a lack of discipline, he would get tired quickly.

After weeks of dedicated study, he thought, "I'm not that bad at getting good grades. This time, if I study for the last three months instead of two, I will still achieve favorable grades." But exactly three months before the exams, he fell ill and lost a crucial month of preparation. Thus, his lack of discipline jeopardized his career.

Therefore, starting today, begin working on your physical discipline by taking up small intentions. This will soon build the capability within you to succeed in all areas of life.

2. Avoid getting entangled in mental roadblocks

Just as a tiny wooden splinter pierces and becomes lodged in the skin of our finger, nature immediately tries to expel it, causing us pain until it is removed. Similarly, nature wishes our minds to be free of the mental splinters they harbor, such as fear, hatred, jealousy, and other buried emotions that hinder our ability to enhance our competence. Hence, nature presents us with opportunities through varied situations to free ourselves from these flaws forever and overcome these mental roadblocks.

Being able to handle such emotions properly is a true sign of competence, as many people become overwhelmed and give up on their goals. They remain unhappy and make everyone around them unhappy. Therefore, to enhance your competence, learn to see every incident as an opportunity to identify your flaws and strive to maintain equanimity despite them.

To achieve this, learn to observe yourself with detachment, as if you were outside the situation. It is similar to how you offer appropriate advice to your friends facing problems but struggle to resolve your own issues due to emotional entanglement. When you look at a situation with detachment, you can clearly see the event, the problem, and its solution, which increases your mental maturity. Once you are convinced that every incident is an opportunity to enhance your competence and evolve, you will learn to stay calm and stable in every situation.

3. Avoid getting swept away by the storms of the mind

Often, a surge of emotions arises within us, leaving us apprehensive and hesitant in our efforts to enhance our competence. For instance, when sorrow descends, our mind is flooded with sorrowful thoughts, creating a cycle of suffering. However, we fail to realize that it is our own tendency to cling to these emotions that disrupts our mental stability. Similarly, when we rejoice in any situation, the mind again entangles us, diverting our focus from our goals. However, this is precisely the time when we must focus on nurturing our qualities, rather than being swept away by the storm of emotions. Only then can we attain inner peace, unshaken by any mental storm.

Anuja, too, could have been swayed by the fun and frolic her friends were enjoying if she had not been guided properly. In the journey of enhancing competence, you will encounter such fleeting pleasures that will try to derail your progress. But learn to give them up so you can achieve true, lasting happiness later. If Anuja had not sought advice from her mother and opted for the short-term pleasures with her friends, she, too, would have encountered a life of sorrow, hardship, and stress, just like them. But since she gave up momentary, short-term pleasures at the right time and chose hard work, she was able to build a life filled with lasting comfort, loving relationships, respect, and confidence.

To make yourself capable of such a contented life, adopt a powerful mantra: **"Sacrifice temporary pleasures for lasting happiness."** Repeat this mantra whenever comforts and fleeting pleasures tempt you. Learn to let go of petty, false pleasures for greater, true happiness.

Remember that obstacles, much like passing clouds, are transient. Therefore, even when obstacles arise, stay focused and maintain steady progress. By mastering your emotional entanglements, cultivating discipline, and overcoming your tendencies, you not only enhance your competence but also experience profound confidence and lasting inner peace.

7

The Competence Mantra

Ashish was watching the busy street below from his small balcony, but he was lost in his own thoughts. After completing his master's degree in business management, he started working at a company. Still, he often dreamed of opening a fusion café that would serve traditional Indian food with a modern twist. He had the vision, plans written in his notebook, and potential locations in his mind, yet he had not taken the first step.

It wasn't a lack of resources that was holding him back. He had enough savings to start and realize his dream. It was his deep-seated self-doubt that stopped him and tormented him every day: "Will I be able to manage everything? What if I fail? Won't people laugh at me? Will they ridicule me?"

Every evening, after returning from work, he would watch the news on TV. One night, he watched an interview with a businessman who had started a small business on a very modest scale and gradually expanded it into a large enterprise. One of his statements struck Ashish deeply: "Initially, I was doubtful whether I would make it." He continued to listen to him intently, as this resonated strongly with him; it reflected his own inner struggle.

The businessman continued, “But my self-doubt eventually turned into confidence as I reached out to fellow entrepreneurs. I learned and understood how they had set up their businesses, how they managed them, and the skills they possessed. I attended courses to acquire the qualities I lacked, read business guidebooks, and consistently networked with people. Gradually, I began to believe I was ready to start my business, and everything began to fall into place smoothly.”

Inspired by the interview, Ashish explored the biographies of successful entrepreneurs, like Dr. Ratan Tata, Dhirubhai Ambani of Reliance Industries, Howard Schultz of Starbucks, Ray Kroc of McDonald’s, Sam Walton of Walmart, and Dr. Verghese Kurien of Amul. Then, he decided to start his own business. He visited some local restaurants and spoke with their managers. He shared his business ideas with his close friends, who encouraged him and even promised to help with marketing.

Gradually, his fear subsided, giving way to a growing sense of confidence. With a mix of apprehension and hope, he applied for the permit required to open the restaurant, drafted his fusion-themed menu, ordered unique fusion-style furniture, and began recruiting staff. As things progressed, his belief in himself grew stronger.

Six months later, Ashish’s fusion café opened its doors and received rave reviews. Dishes like Tacos and spiced Chai Lattes at his café became instant hits. Word spread, and soon his café became a favorite among locals and tourists.

Ashish felt a deep sense of pride and satisfaction. He began mentoring others and sharing the importance of confidence with those who were struggling with self-doubt. His journey became a beacon of hope and inspiration for those who, just like him, needed a little push to move forward.

Ashish had the potential to become a successful entrepreneur, but his fear of failure, fueled by self-doubt, held him back. After reading many books and talking with people from different backgrounds, he began to feel courage within himself; his competence and faith grew, and eventually his self-doubt disappeared like camphor.

Pause for a moment and reflect: Do you also feel, "I can't do this, I can't do that?" Do you want to unlock your hidden, untapped potential? It might not require starting a new business or getting a new job; it could simply be about being competent and proficient in what you already do. If so, cast aside your self-doubt by understanding the Competence Mantra.

If you look closely, everyone already has inherent capabilities that are often hidden for some reason. Life offers several opportunities to enhance their capabilities by developing their skills and qualities. However, most often, they cannot fully blossom due to self-doubt. Therefore, to boost your confidence, use the Competence Mantra: **"Competence is always present within."**

In essence, competence is always within you; it is ready to open up. You just need to recognize it and hone it to bring it out. When you feel less confident or doubtful about yourself while performing a task, affirm to yourself: "Competence is always present within; I just need to bring it out."

Along with repeating the mantra, you can also practice contemplation and writing. It is an effective way to identify your self-doubts and address them.

Begin by listing the things you currently believe you cannot do. For example, "I can't speak in English fluently. I can't speak in front of everyone in meetings. I don't know how to use a computer or a laptop. I can't perform some yoga postures. I don't know Pranayama. I can't dance. I don't know Sanskrit. I can't drive. I can't blow a whistle. I can't snap my fingers and so on." These are just a few examples.

Write down 101 things you believe you cannot do in your diary. Then, for each item, write down specific steps you can take to overcome that self-doubt. For example, you might join a class, seek advice from someone, read a relevant book, cultivate a new habit, or develop a new skill.

Now, before writing in your diary, list at least 11 self-doubt-related thoughts in the chart below.

Sr. No.	**Your self-doubts Tasks you feel you cannot do**	**Steps you will take to do them**
1.	I am afraid to talk to people.	I will begin conversing with people.
2.	I do not know how to operate the computer.	I will enroll in a computer class to learn.
3.	I cannot speak in English.	I will sign up for an English-speaking class to improve.
4.	I cannot do much work; I lack stamina and endurance.	I will incorporate yoga into my routine to build my stamina.
5.		
6.		
7.		
8.		
9.		
10.		
11.		

Every necessary capability already exists within you, but because you are unaware of it, you do not see yourself as worthy of it, and you doubt yourself. When you write down your self-doubts and how you plan to develop that capability, nature provides the strength to grow and build it. So, without hesitation, record your self-doubts and growth plans to overcome your doubts and reveal the competence within you.

8

Strengthen Your Foundation

In a small village, there was a poor man named Dhananand. One day, a well-known and revered saint visited his village. Dhananand served him tirelessly, hoping for a better future and relief from his hardships. The saint, pleased with his selfless service, asked, "What is it that you wish for?" Dhananand humbly replied, "Please grant me relief from this life of poverty."

The saint handed him five lamps and instructed, "Light one of these, and walk north. When its flame flickers out, dig there, and you will find wealth. If you need more wealth, light another lamp and walk south. For future needs, light another and go east. For more need, light the fourth lamp and go west. But mind my words: Never use the fifth lamp and never go near any ruins."

The saint then departed, leaving Dhananand with a heart full of hope. He eagerly lit the first lamp and headed north. Where the flame flickered out, he dug and discovered a treasure of riches. He returned home overjoyed.

After a few days, he thought, "Let this wealth get exhausted, then I'll go in another direction." But then another thought overwhelmed him, "Why wait? I'll go now." Driven by greed, he lit the second lamp and journeyed south. He found a great deal of wealth there as well. Now, he became more voracious. He lit the third lamp and went east. He kept finding more wealth everywhere, and his hunger for more knew no end. So, he also went west and found even more.

Now, he looked at the fifth lamp and wondered, "There's some secret about this one. The saint has hidden something from me that he doesn't want me to have. Why did he tell me not to light this lamp and warn me against going near any ruins?" Unable to resist, he set out in search of the ruins.

Eventually, he found the ruins and lit the fifth lamp to enter. Once inside, he saw a magnificent palace. He thought, "I've come to the right place. I'll find some great treasure here." When he stepped into the palace, he saw an old man turning a mill to grind flour. He went to him and asked, "Who are you? And why are you turning this mill here?"

The old man looked up and replied, "I am the guardian of this treasure. There's indeed a vast treasure here."

Dhananand exclaimed happily, "Oh, really! Tell me, I've come for that treasure! The saint has blessed me, and now I'm here."

The old man said, "I've been turning this mill for a long time, and I'm tired. I'll tell you everything, including my own story. But first, while I rest a bit, keep the mill turning. The mill shouldn't stop, or else the palace will collapse on you."

Dhananand happily agreed and began turning the mill. The old man lay down to rest, closing his eyes in apparent relief. Time passed, but when he didn't get up for a long time, Dhananand impatiently called out, "Hey! Get up, brother. How long will you rest? Tell me quickly, where is the treasure?"

The old man replied, "I'm coming!" He returned after taking a stroll around the palace and said, "I'm leaving now. Keep grinding the mill. I, too, had received five lamps. I came here seeking treasure but got trapped instead. Now, I am leaving but remember not to stop grinding; otherwise, the palace will collapse on you. I've been grinding this mill out of fear for all these days and years."

Dhananand froze and grew apprehensive; he had not expected this. With his eyes wide with despair, he asked, "So, I'm trapped now. But before you go, tell me when and how I will be free from this?" The old man replied with a sorrowful smile, "Only when someone with a weak foundation comes like you. Until then, you will not be liberated. You should do to them what I did to you; only then will you be free."

Dhananand had been poor, but his life, though humble, was going on well, and most importantly, he was free and at peace. However, when tempted by wealth, his foundation shook, his roots weakened, and caught up in greed, he became a prisoner for life—a slave to it.

Similarly, people driven by greed often compromise their integrity. They lie, deceive, and resort to unethical practices to gain name, fame, position, and wealth. However, this weakens their foundation, erodes their competence, and leads to negative consequences in their lives. Soon, they realize that the name, fame, position, and wealth they have earned are transient and were gained at the cost of their inner strength, credibility, and peace.

A strong foundation involves having solid, unfaltering ideals and noble guiding principles in life, ethics, and moral values. When we live according to certain principles, adopt specific values, and make decisions in line with them, we strengthen the foundation of our life. Principles serve as a moral inheritance that helps us discern right from wrong. They guide us to understand that to succeed in life, we should avoid unethical practices, shortcuts, or deceit. Instead, we should uphold these principles to fortify our foundation, build our character, and improve the quality of our life and our competence.

Therefore, if you wish to enhance your competence, you need to build a strong foundation. This involves being honest and sincere, maintaining integrity, understanding and managing your emotions, especially anger, and avoiding harmful addictions like alcohol. We all know these principles; we just need to fully embrace them.

Decide what you will remind yourself of when a desire for money tempts you and how you will respond when you feel angry. You might resolve to get angry only once a week. You could set specific times each week for watching TV or using your phone for entertainment. This will not only help you control your phone and TV usage but also improve your time management skills. Similarly, you might set principles not to take loans to show off false pride, not to achieve success through shortcuts, not to cheat on exams, or to participate in unethical business practices. With this, you can stay aware of these temptations even amid materialistic allurements and avoid getting caught up in them.

For example, a new weekend trend has emerged lately, including watching movies, shopping at malls, staying at luxury resorts, and dining out. Some people started this trend, and many, influenced by social pressure or the lure of indulgence, followed suit, often spending beyond their means and leading to ongoing financial problems. They see this as the only way to enjoy life. However, they rarely pause to realize that it is a waste of time and money, and they inadvertently pass these values on to their children.

Instead, they can choose to spend quality time with their families. This might include visiting elderly relatives, playing games with children, engaging in drawing and crafts, and sharing traditional activities with the younger generation. Doing so not only strengthens their bond but also fosters healthier relationships and helps maintain financial stability. When love and respect are present in relationships, along with happiness, contentment, and peace at home, it reflects the quality of their lives. These values and this strong foundation are passed down to children as a legacy through the example set by their parents.

Once your principles are established, no temptation or external situation can shake or weaken your foundation because your reasoning and understanding of how to handle them are clear. Such a strong foundation not only reinforces your trustworthiness but also enhances your competence.

9

The Secret of Achieving Desired Outcomes

Vishal sat at his desk, with his fingers still on the keyboard, staring at the blank computer screen, mirroring the emptiness he felt within. For the past five years, he had been working in the same position, hoping for a promotion that never came through. One by one, his colleagues advanced to the next position while he remained stuck in the same position.

It wasn't that Vishal lacked ambition; rather, each time he tried to prove himself, he ended up making mistakes. He struggled with giving presentations; his ideas often lacked depth, and he always succumbed to pressure.

Besides his career, Vishal's physical health also declined. Once an avid runner, he now struggled to climb even a flight of stairs without panting. His mornings often began with good intentions, such as planning workouts and a healthy breakfast. But more often, they ended with sweetened coffee and skipping workouts. He would promise himself, "I will surely do it tomorrow," but never kept the promise. His habit of procrastination contributed to his lack of discipline.

Vishal's personal life bore testimony to his professional and health struggles. His friends had stopped reaching out to him. "You are always either too busy or distracted," his best friend Manas told him during their last conversation. At home, things were no better. He had a strained relationship with his wife, Meena. She would always point out his shortcomings. "It's like you're here, but your mind seems elsewhere," she said one evening, her face writ with disappointment.

One evening, Vishal was alone at home. When he washed his face and looked in the mirror, he saw an old, tired face with sunken eyes staring back at him. The reflection seemed older than his thirty-five years. A wave of remorse washed over him. "Where has that young man, full of dreams and energy, gone? Where has it all gone wrong?" The answer was a stark, painful truth: In every unfinished project, every broken promise, and every goal that had been carelessly abandoned without challenge, his former self had gradually disappeared.

Vishal realized it wasn't fate or some cosmic conspiracy that had landed him in this situation. It was his lack of discipline, flexibility, and competence in learning and progressing further. He had spent years waiting for things to change without taking any action to make them happen.

With this realization, he resolved to take small but deliberate steps to change himself. He enrolled in a public speaking class to address his professional shortcomings. Instead of eating fast food, he opted for a healthy lunch. To mend his relationships, he first sought forgiveness from his loved ones and then promised to make things right.

Things didn't go well. He stumbled through his first public speaking class, the healthy food tasted bland, and people's responses were lukewarm, but he persevered. For the first time in years, he saw a glimmer of hope, not because his circumstances had changed, but because he finally decided to change himself. The only way left was up from the abyss of depair.

Vishal's journey was far from over. But he had learned a valuable lesson: The desired outcomes in life don't come solely from hope and desire but also from effort, perseverance, resilience, and the courage to confront his own shortcomings. Although the road ahead was long, he had now come to understand that he had the strength to shape his future, one step at a time.

Like Vishal, everyone dreams of a happy, successful, and fulfilled life. However, many fail to realize these dreams and face setbacks. They aim to reach certain heights in different areas of their lives but often fall short.

Pause for a moment and reflect: Why might this be happening? Why do some dreams take flight while others fade away?

"Whatever we become competent and worthy of inevitably comes into our life." According to this principle, everything we have in our life today is because we have become capable of receiving it. This might include a good education, a rewarding career, good health, financial stability, respect, loving relationships, or a happy, contented family. It also means that whatever we have longed for but have not yet achieved are because we have not yet become capable and worthy of having them.

In essence, if we are unable to achieve a desired outcome in any area of life, we must improve our sense of worthiness and our capability to attain it. We need to identify the skills and qualities we lack to achieve those things.

Does this resonate with your life as well? Are you struggling to fulfill some of your dreams? Are you unable to achieve the desired results in some areas of your life? If so, you should contemplate the qualities and skills you need to develop and enhance to realize your dreams. Create a plan of action and start working toward it. Even small steps matter, because just like a pond fills drop by drop, each small step will gradually lead you toward fulfilling your dreams.

Here is the first step of introspection. Reflect on the areas of your life where you are not achieving the outcomes you desire. The following is a reference list. Introspect, identify, and tick (✓) the relevant areas. Remember, only when you become capable and worthy will those things come in your life.

1. Higher education ☐
2. Career - a fulfilling job or a successful business ☐
3. Promotion or higher position ☐
4. Financial stability ☐
5. Harmonious relationships ☐
6. Vitality and well-being ☐

In the forthcoming chapters, we will explore some stories to understand the qualities that can enhance your capabilities to achieve any goal and their importance. This will help you reflect on them, take small yet impactful steps to develop these qualities, and make you worthy of realizing each of your dreams.

PART 2

YOUR EVOLVED FORM ENDOWED WITH 12 VIRTUES

10

The Power of Resolve

"I am leaving all of you forever.
Yes! I know this decision is wrong, but I have no other option left.

You have brought me up with so much love and care,
but I couldn't live up to it.
Please forgive me if you can.

- Your Seema."

It was nearly midnight. Under the faint glow of her bedside lamp, Seema was writing a desperate note to her parents and beloved brother, Sham. As she signed her name, her mind weighed down by unspoken grief, the pen slipped from her trembling fingers. After quietly staring into the void for a few moments, she couldn't hold back any longer, and tears of guilt rolled down her cheeks.

After a few moments, she wiped away her tears, strengthened her resolve, and tiptoed toward the door. She was cautious, lest even the slightest noise might wake up her family, who were fast asleep, unaware of her decision. She paused briefly to look at them one last time. Then, she reached the door and slowly unlatched it. Taking a deep, shuddering breath, she gently closed the door and slipped out into the night. She began walking toward the railway station.

Seema lived in a small town. She was a well-behaved, modest, and hardworking young woman. After completing her graduation at the age of twenty-one, she wanted to advance her career. Since childhood, she had dreamed of becoming a beauty therapist. However, her parents were eager to see her married after graduation and be free from their duty.

No sooner were her final exam results announced than her parents began looking for a suitable match for her. Seeing this, Seema felt as if her dreams for the future were beginning to crumble. She was deeply disappointed. Every day, the local priest brought new marriage proposals from nearby villages, and Seema was presented in front of prospective grooms, an experience that made her feel suffocated. She lacked the courage to voice her opinion to her father and couldn't endure such restrictions either. So, silently and painfully, she decided to run away from home and reclaim her future on her own terms.

Wrapped in a shawl, she slipped through the darkness. At the train station, she bought a ticket for the first train heading toward the city. She settled onto a cold, steel bench, the silence broken only by the distant rumble of an approaching train.

As the train screeched to a halt, she boarded swiftly, seeking refuge in a quiet corner. The train lurched forward, and as its speed increased, her thoughts also raced. She shuddered at the chaos her departure would unleash upon her family at dawn and her uncertain future.

As she was lost in her whirlwind of thoughts, she was startled by a sudden touch on her shoulder. She instinctively raised her hand in defense out of unknown fear, but when she looked up, she was stunned. She had never in her wildest dreams imagined meeting her on the train. She immediately stood up and touched her feet in reverence. It was Vidya, her favorite tenth-grade teacher—a figure from her cherished past. Vidya, in turn, placed her comforting hand on Seema's head with concern.

Seema had always been Vidya's favorite student. Feeling her teacher's motherly touch on her head, Seema couldn't hold back her emotions and burst into tears. Unable to understand Seema's state, Vidya gently sat beside her. After a while, when Seema calmed down, she recounted the entire story of her desperate escape.

Vidya thought for a moment and then said, in a gentle yet firm voice, "My dear, the Seema I knew was a brave girl. I fail to understand your act of running away in the middle of the night without telling anyone. Do you remember the stories I told all of you in school to boost your confidence? They were meant to motivate you to face real-life challenges courageously rather than running away from them."

"Yes, I remember," Seema whispered, her shoulders slumping as she looked down. "But the situation was so overwhelming that I am convinced I had no other choice."

In a reassuring tone, Vidya explained to her, "We face many difficult situations in life. However, we must embrace the quality of standing up and facing them instead of fleeing. When we resolve to confront every challenge, we find the solution to every problem."

"But I couldn't find a solution to my problem," Seema pleaded, her voice heavy with despair. "My parents will never understand my point."

"Have you ever tried to explain it to them?" Vidya asked, her gaze piercing. Seema was lost for words because she had never tried to discuss it with her parents; she had simply assumed it was pointless to talk to them.

Sensing her silence, Vidya continued, "Seema, whenever you face a problem in life, don't ever think about escaping it. Escaping doesn't solve problems but only makes them worse. Instead, firmly resolve to find a solution to your problem, and you will surely find a way forward. You are so capable; speaking to your parents shouldn't be so hard for you."

Seema agreed, "Yes, I know I can convey my point to others, but still, I don't understand why I ran away."

Vidya replied softly, a gentle smile on her face, "It's because you never truly reflected on how to stand up and face this situation. Otherwise, you always accomplish what you firmly resolve to do."

Seema nodded in agreement. Vidya continued, "When we firmly resolve to find a solution to a problem, positive energy stirs within us; our thoughts and actions are channeled in the right direction. It's like a farmer; only when they resolve to grow a crop do they feel motivated to sow seeds, toil hard, and tend to the harvest. If they give up in the beginning, thinking the crop won't grow or there will be challenges, they won't accomplish anything. Similarly, your resolve is the very foundation of your next steps.

"Remember, we can find a solution to any problem only when we accept it and resolve to confront it. Escaping neither solves the problem nor relieves the stress. But when we bolster our resolve with courage, solutions begin to appear naturally. Just think about how you want to improve your life and also keep your parents happy. You can find a solution to your problem by walking this path together with them."

Seema listened to Vidya's words attentively. She realized she had truly given up without trying her best. She silently resolved not to escape her problems, but to go home and talk to her parents.

"You are absolutely right," she said, in a firm and clear voice. "I promise to confront my problems and seek solutions to them."

Vidya smiled with satisfaction and said, "That's the spirit! Remember, there is no greater power than resolve and confidence. Therefore, instead of escaping from the problem, it's better to analyze it and take the right steps at the right time to find a solution. For instance, if your parents disagree with you, change the way you communicate with them. If verbal communication can cause confrontation, you may even resort to written communication. If that doesn't work, seek help from a trusted relative. If that too fails, speak to the potential grooms who come to see you. You've heard the saying, 'Those who try never fail.' By taking the right steps with complete faith, you can easily find a solution to every problem."

It had been five years since that incident. Today, Seema was getting married to a doctor from a reputed family. She had also become a successful beauty therapist. Her parents felt happy and proud of their decision. The memory of the five-year-old incident flashed before them.

That night, after thanking her teacher, Seema got off at the next train station. A renewed sense of determination and a glimmer of hope filled her heart. She bought a ticket for the next train on the opposite platform, boarded the train, and headed home.

It was nearly dawn when Seema quietly slipped into her house. Everyone was still asleep. She noticed the letter she had written lying untouched. She quickly tore it up, changed her clothes, and went to sleep. In the morning, everyone woke up and began their chores. In the evening, when her parents were together, Seema shared everything that had happened that night. They were stunned and a little worried that Seema might take such a step again.

Seema hugged her mother and reassured her parents, "Don't worry, I won't do it again." Her mother, looking at her compassionately with a mix of love and relief in her eyes, said, "God bless your teacher. The step you took last night was wrong. But with your teacher's guidance, you have now learned that living a life of escape is not wise. We have full faith that no matter what comes in the future, you will confront every problem head-on and resolve it positively without running away."

Although her father seemed strict on the outside, he deeply loved Seema. He told her, "Your teacher was right. I am grateful to her for showing you the light. I also realize that my narrow-minded thinking made me believe that a grown-up daughter belongs to someone else's family and that she should be married off quickly, so I can be done with my duty. In reality, a daughter should be empowered to be self-reliant before getting married so that, instead of relying on someone else, she can become a support for others when needed."

Seema was awestruck by the way the whole scene unfolded; the seemingly major problem was easily solved through effective communication. And even if it hadn't been solved, she was prepared to confront it. With her father's approval, she firmly decided to progress in her career, worked hard, and soon achieved success. Freedom from escapism and the power of firm resolve made her life fulfilling and worthwhile.

Understanding and Insight

This story teaches us an important lesson: **"Never invite an anaconda to escape an ant."** Essentially, do not invite a bigger disaster to avoid a minor discomfort. Instead, embrace the power of firm resolve and face challenges bravely to succeed.

Often, the habit of escapism takes root in childhood. When parents overly pamper their children, children learn to withdraw and develop the habit of escapism. For example, if a child scatters their toys while playing, the mother might ask the maid to tidy them up. The child observes such small incidents and unconsciously learns to avoid responsibilities. As they grow older, this pattern continues. They begin to avoid tasks given by their mother or important schoolwork, or they procrastinate by thinking, "I'll do it later."

Similarly, when the toy they are playing with gets slightly damaged, the child might, without even trying to fix it, leave it and pick up another one. If they dislike a particular food, they avoid it. By doing these things repeatedly, they develop the habit of escaping problems and challenges.

Remember, life will inevitably bring challenges, but only by facing them head-on can we discover a new way forward. For this, we must have a firm resolve to confront challenges first and then develop the skills and capabilities to overcome them.

Forming a resolve is the first step toward changing your mindset and outlook on life. It is like a seed that can grow into a tree of solutions. When you resolve to confront a challenge, you give it priority. This reduces confusion in your mind, allowing you to focus on the solution rather than the problem itself and channel your energy in the right way.

Action plan:

Take a diary and note down five situations where you feel uncomfortable and a strong urge to escape. Now, ask yourself, "What resolute intention can I take to find a solution?" You can follow these three steps to arrive at your resolve.

1. Clearly state your problem. In Lakshmi's case, she was unable to communicate with her parents, assuming they would not understand her.
2. Create a positive and firm resolve. For example, "I must talk openly with my parents." Alternatively, write down your feelings and ask for help in a letter.
3. Create a simple and effective action plan. For instance, Lakshmi decided to talk frankly with her parents.

Reflect on these three steps and jot down your insights in the diary. Take the actions you feel are right at the moment and boldly face the situation. Start working on it and see what unfolds.

11

Maintaining Consistency

Since childhood, Ajay had dreamed of accomplishing something remarkable. He had envisioned himself growing up to be a proficient and successful badminton player. Since he was twelve, he had regularly competed in badminton tournaments at his school and in his neighborhood, often winning and celebrating his victories. His height and unique playing style gave him an edge over his competitors. Besides sports, he also excelled academically, so his parents fully supported his passion for the sport.

However, as he moved on to senior college and won a few medals in local competitions, his pride got the better of him. Little did he realize that his confidence had morphed into arrogance, leading him to spend less time on his practice. Additionally, hanging out with his friends also adversely affected his focus and discipline.

Gradually, his performance in tournaments began to decline. However, he ignored it, thinking, "What's the big deal if I lose a game or two?" He didn't change his routine, unaware that his complacency was eroding the very foundation of his success.

One day, Ajay participated in a tournament at the City Sports Club. Ajay's childhood coach, Vijay Singh, was the referee for that match. When in school, he had taught Ajay some excellent techniques of the game that could have taken him way ahead. However, watching Ajay's performance that day, Vijay Singh was totally disappointed. Ajay lost the match and felt disheartened that he couldn't win despite playing so well. He went to meet his coach after the game.

After a casual chat, Vijay Singh finally asked him, "Ajay, where is your focus these days? Your performance isn't what it used to be. How many days a week and how many hours a day do you practice? Have you even set a big goal for this sport?"

Hearing his barrage of questions, Ajay's eyes dropped in embarrassment as he had no answers. He could only mumble, "I, too, can't understand what has suddenly changed in my game; why my performance has deteriorated. I always wanted to be the number one badminton player in the country, just like you."

Vijay Singh was once an international champion, having won gold medals at the Asian Games. He was aware of Ajay's potential, which only needed sharpening. He knew where Ajay was falling short but chose not to tell him at that moment. Instead, he advised him to analyze his own game and work on improving it, then left.

Ajay felt put off by the way his coach left without pointing out his mistakes.

He sat by a riverbank, trying to analyze his defeat. He was steeped in memories of the last game he lost. Despair cast a dark shadow over his mind. He couldn't figure out what to do next. Just then, his eyes fell on a small, murky puddle nearby filled with water. The stagnant water was teeming with insects. He wondered why the water in this puddle was so dirty.

He watched the puddle for a while, then looked at the river. The river's water was clean and clear, flowing constantly. Its waves seemed to whisper something to him. He noticed that the river water stays clean because it flows continuously. If it were to stop, it would also become foul like the water in the puddle.

With this realization, Ajay began reflecting on past incidents. He realized the critical role of consistency and unwavering dedication in achieving success. He regretted, "Had I also kept practicing without a break, I wouldn't have faced this defeat today."

He finally understood that consistent learning was required for maintaining his competence, and his success lay hidden in his persistent practice, just as the purity of river water lies in its continuous flow.

This realization ignited a spark within him, lighting up his face with renewed energy and confidence. He resolved never to give up. With this firm resolve and a flicker of new dreams in his eyes, he set out to meet his coach.

Ajay told his coach, "You have coached me since my childhood, but when I entered college, my practice dwindled. As a result, I lost the last three to four matches in a row, which also waned my confidence. But now, I would like to train with you again."

The coach agreed to train him on the condition that Ajay would have to undergo training exactly as instructed; he would need to diligently adhere to his training regimen and stay committed to his scheduled practice hours. Ajay was more than willing to accept all his conditions as the sting of repeated failures had left him deeply disappointed.

The next day, when Ajay arrived at the badminton club, the coach first took away his mobile phone and said, "This phone is the biggest obstacle on your path toward your goal. You're allowed to use it for an hour daily until you become a top-level champion.

You must refrain from using it during training or competition." Ajay had firmly resolved that he would not give up hereafter. He gave his word to the coach and committed himself to fulfilling it wholeheartedly.

The next morning, the coach summoned Ajay to the club lawn at 5:00 a.m. and assigned him a strict regimen. This included an hour of running and jumping exercises, an hour of gym workout, and four hours of badminton practice. A month passed, and Ajay diligently followed this regimen.

Observing Ajay's progress, one day the coach remarked with a smile, "A lack of consistency was the cause for your defeat. Now that you are becoming adept at maintaining it, no one can stop you from succeeding."

Ajay nodded in agreement. The coach continued, "You know we can attain ultimate success and achieve any goal in any field when we fully embrace consistency. Whether you win or lose, you should never abandon your training midway. I can see that consistent practice has now become an integral part of your routine. You must keep progressing in this manner from now on."

Ajay continued his training wholeheartedly, embracing consistency. Over the next three months, he enhanced his agility and flexibility by acquiring advanced techniques under Vijay Singh's guidance. Consequently, winning city-level tournaments became easier for him. He won the district and state-level tournaments within six months and was selected to play at the national level.

When Ajay won his first national championship medal, the coach said with great pride, "This is just the beginning. You must rise to the highest level through disciplined and consistent practice. Always remember this goal. My blessings are with you."

Ajay bowed down gratefully, touched his coach's feet, and adopted the principle of consistency as the guiding force for his life. Following in his coach's footsteps, he also rose to become a successful international player.

Understanding and Insight

"Consistency is the key to extraordinary success." It is a quality that plays a crucial role in helping anyone reach their goals.

When we consistently pursue a goal, we move closer to success. Consistency instils discipline in us, keeps us committed to our goals, and helps us overcome our weaknesses.

However, consistency does not mean working relentlessly; it means putting in regular effort to reach our goals. The key aspect of consistency is that it makes us resilient even in the face of hardship. While pursuing our goal, we often face challenges. Consistency empowers us to tackle them and stay on the right track. Therefore, if we aspire for extraordinary success, we must make consistency an integral part of our lives. It will help improve the quality of our lives.

Action plan:

We often enthusiastically start a task but lose interest after a few days. So, challenge yourself to stay consistent with any task.

The following are a few ways to stay consistent in your efforts:

1. **Challenge yourself:** Select a task you want to stay consistent with. Commit to it for at least seven or fifteen days in a row. If you miss even one day, you have to start all over again, counting the next day as Day One. In this way, complete your first challenge of seven or fifteen days. Then, take a break for one or two days and start with a new challenge for seven or fifteen days. Track your progress on a calendar to ensure you do not miss a single day. This helps maintain your consistency, and you will not feel bored by taking periodical breaks.
2. **Start with small steps:** If you decide to walk regularly, avoid walking too far at first. Walk one kilometer for the first three to four days. Add another ten meters next week. Gradually, increase

the distance by about ten meters each week. This way, you will enjoy walking and will not feel exhausted. Walk five days a week and rest for two days. This balanced routine will help you stay consistent.

3. **Analyze your daily routine:** Examine your daily routine and identify the gap between your thoughts about a goal and the actions you take toward it. How can you bridge this gap by maintaining consistency?

   Write down five tasks where your mind makes excuses, struggles to stay consistent, and keeps procrastinating. These tasks could include cleaning the house, making repairs, fulfilling office responsibilities, improving health, or pursuing spiritual growth.

4. **Seek external support:** You can also improve your consistency with the help of others. For example, if you have decided to read a book every month but tend to procrastinate every day, consider joining a friend or a group of avid readers. You can use a mobile app to track your progress. When you notice its benefits, you will feel motivated to continue, and regular reading will become part of your daily routine.

By embracing consistency, you can experience remarkable changes in your life. Begin today and continue moving forward toward your goals.

12

The Art of Learning

Mohit grew up in a wealthy family where comfort and luxury were part of everyday life. Even if he did nothing, his family's wealth guaranteed a comfortable life for generations. However, Mohit didn't enjoy living this way. As a child, while other children were busy playing sports and games, Mohit developed a hobby of cooking.

His culinary journey started in school with a weekly cooking class. While his peers reluctantly dragged themselves there, Mohit's face would light up with excitement. He began with simple savory treats, like chocolate cake, pasta, and pancakes. However, as he grew older, his hobby turned into a passion. He took great pleasure in creating new recipes and presenting them in a unique style.

However, Mohit's parents disapproved of his interest in cooking. They repeatedly told him, "This is more suited for girls. When we have servants to manage the kitchen, why are you wasting your time there?" They considered it a frivolous pursuit. But their words couldn't stop him. He remained undeterred and kept pursuing his passion.

However, Mohit had a significant shortcoming: he couldn't stand his own criticism. He believed he was always right and disliked anyone correcting him. His stubbornness became the biggest obstacle to his progress. While pursuing his chosen path, would Mohit truly live his dream, or would his passion lead him elsewhere?

As the days passed, Mohit kept experimenting with his cooking. Whenever he wanted to try something new, he searched for recipes online. Over time, his dishes got better and tastier. However, neither his family nor his guests gave him any feedback on his cooking; they neither praised nor criticized him. Despite the flaws, everyone quietly ate the food he prepared; no one dared to upset him.

When the household chefs, who had spent years preparing exquisite food, offered any suggestions, Mohit would lose his temper: "Your ideas are outdated. I'm creating modern cuisine. I don't need your advice. Just mind your own business." His harsh words would silence them, and they would quietly step back.

Despite being proficient in theory, Mohit's dream of becoming a great chef remained unfulfilled. He persevered tirelessly, but his cooking still lacked that special touch needed to make him a competent and successful chef.

A new turn came about in Mohit's life when he married Asmita. Asmita was not only tolerant and intelligent but also a composed companion. While she admired Mohit's passion for cooking and his dream of becoming a successful chef, she also saw his inability to learn from his mistakes.

After marriage, Mohit was drawn to Asmita's gentle nature. She was the first person who listened to him and helped him unburden himself without judging. While the rest of his family rebuked him and considered him incompetent, Asmita was growing closer to his heart.

One day, Asmita gently coaxed Mohit with a smile by asking, "Wouldn't you like to treat me to a special dish prepared by you?" Mohit felt elated. He immediately began making carrot pudding for her. Asmita quietly stood by his side, offering support, but she did not utter a word during the process.

When the pudding was ready, they sat down to eat. Mohit immediately realized that the carrot pudding was less sweet and slightly burnt. Yet, Asmita kept quietly eating it. Mohit couldn't stand the silence and blurted out, "The pudding isn't tasty. It's less sweet and burnt. Still, you are eating it. Why aren't you saying anything? What's wrong with you?"

Asmita gently replied, "I've heard that if anyone interrupts you while you're cooking or points out a flaw in the food, you get angry. I didn't want to upset you, so I kept quiet."

"But if you don't tell me, how will I ever know what is missing in the dish?" Mohit asked after a pause. It was the first time he had taken someone's words seriously and expressed a desire to receive feedback.

Asmita looked at him and said, "If you're ready to take feedback, I'd like to share a few things with you." Mohit immediately nodded in agreement.

"If a speck of dust gets into your eye, you can't see it yourself, but someone else can clearly spot it and remove it," she began. "Similarly, others can see more of our flaws than we do. Hence, we should always be open to feedback because it helps us learn faster and improve."

She continued, "When I was about to get married, my parents advised me, 'The circumstances ahead may be different from what you've learned or preferred here. But if you carry the art of learning with you, you will soon win everyone's heart there.' So, after coming here, I started learning a lot, even about the way you all live. I began observing everyone's qualities and learning from them, which helped me get along with everyone by setting aside my initial resistance. It is solely because of this ability to learn that my life is progressing smoothly with you."

Her words deeply touched Mohit. No one had ever explained to him with such humility and maturity before. He realized the profound importance of learning and the value of accepting feedback.

Asmita was a skilled cook herself and had also attended a professional cooking course. She began exploring new dishes with Mohit and gradually taught him some effective and useful cooking techniques. Her understanding and patience boosted his confidence.

Eventually, Mohit opened an upscale restaurant, making his dream come true. He found success and fulfillment by turning his passion into a thriving reality. His life took a positive turn when he embraced the art of learning and diligently corrected his mistakes. Asmita taught him that the master key to lasting progress is a powerful blend of humility and an unyielding will to learn.

Understanding and Insight

When one possesses the quality of learning, their inner resistance begins to dissolve. By letting go of the rigid mindset of "I know" or "I know better," their focus shifts to learning new things and enhancing their competence. The art of learning is a quality that helps us overcome all obstacles and challenges. It propels us forward on a path of continuous growth, leading us to the pinnacle of success.

Action plan:

1. **Learning from mistakes:** To err is human; to learn, divine. Perfection is a myth, while our mistakes offer a fertile ground for growth. Making mistakes is not wrong, but failing to learn from them is. We must analyze our mistakes, understand their root causes, and learn lessons from them so we do not repeat them.
2. **Accepting feedback:** Others often perceive our mistakes or weaknesses more clearly than we do because we view ourselves from a fixed and limited perspective, while they see us from an external, broader perspective. So, when someone points out our flaws, we should accept it gracefully as a blessing. Feedback is a valuable resource that helps us bring about transformation and live a better, improved life.
3. **Committing to consistent learning: "I will keep learning as long as I live."** This commitment motivates us to keep learning throughout our lives. Regardless of our age, the learning process always keeps us youthful because it makes us enthusiastic and aware of new things.
4. **Experimenting and being aware:** Staying aware and continuously experimenting in life are an integral part of learning. Sometimes, when we act without complete information, mistakes are inevitable. But instead of regretting these mistakes and giving up, we should learn from them and keep moving forward.

The art of learning is the most important quality that steers our life in a positive direction. Therefore, never stop the process of learning and strive to gain new insights at every turn, in every experience of life, reaching the pinnacle of competence.

13

Embracing Flexibility

Santosh was a young, ambitious man whose luck had recently been in his favor. He got a job as an Assistant Manager in a shopping mall. The moment he received the job offer, his excitement soared sky-high. He thought a manager's job meant sitting in a comfortable office, issuing orders to everyone, and supervising their work. He expected it to be an easy and relaxed job.

The first few days went precisely as he had expected. Everything in the environment felt refreshing to him. However, as the Diwali season started in the second week, a chaotic situation swept over the mall. The place became a hub of activity, with new stock arriving in large numbers, pending orders demanding fulfillment, and hordes of customers to manage.

And to add to this, Santosh had to pitch in with every task himself. He even had to lift boxes and organize goods, returning home late and exhausted. He couldn't understand why a manager had to toil like a laborer. His dream of effortless bossing was shattered. To make matters worse, his usually calm and patient boss had now started losing his temper and overreacting to trivial issues. Gradually, he felt his job had become a burden.

One night, when he returned home late, completely exhausted, he was surprised to find his father awake. Noticing his tired eyes, his father asked, "Son, is everything alright? You seem disturbed."

Santosh thought to himself, "What do I tell him? He's been a humble schoolteacher; how would he understand this labor-intensive managerial job of mine?" Yet, his father's questions, filled with affection, compelled him to share his story. He explained how unhappy and disappointed he was with his job, how his boss made him work like a laborer.

His father listened to him patiently with a quiet smile, then spoke softly, "Do you remember our walks by the river when you were little? You would watch how the river carved its own path even amid rocks and obstacles. Sometimes, it would become a gentle stream, and at other times a rushing torrent."

Santosh instantly recalled that scene and asked, "Yes, I remember, but what's that got to do with my present situation?"

His father gently replied, "We must be exactly like the river. We should be flexible, and we must learn to adapt ourselves to every situation."

Santosh countered, "Do you mean I should also adapt to any situation, no matter how difficult it may be?!"

His father explained, "Yes. A person who faces every challenge head-on becomes a true leader. They are neither defined by their designation nor by the authority they hold. In a challenging situation, an effective leader doesn't stay on the safe shore and simply issue orders to others to get the job done, but rolls up his sleeves and dives into the thick of activities and works alongside them. Therefore, no matter what the work is, don't hesitate to do it. When the circumstances are tough, consider yourself as water, adapt to every situation, and surrender. Gracefully navigate every situation and move forward, just like a river flowing through the available space without resistance, surrendering to the situation. This is a key lesson of life. Flexibility and adaptability are not signs of weakness but the very essence of leadership. Now, you decide whether you aspire to be just a boss or a true leader."

That night's conversation with his father ignited a spark within Santosh. He resolved not to escape challenges but to confront them and turn them to his advantage. The next day, he went to work with a renewed perspective and energy. He poured his heart into every task. He talked to his colleagues with kindness and empathy, listened to their concerns keenly, and tried to understand them.

Slowly, the Diwali season came to an end, but everyone noticed Santosh's changed behavior. His colleagues began admiring him more than before, and even his boss praised his efforts. Filled with a surge of confidence, he realized he could thrive in any situation by embracing flexibility like water.

This valuable experience steered him in a new direction. Now, he no longer considered himself just an assistant store manager, but began to think and act like a true leader. He learned that real strength lies in turning any adversity into an advantage, thus preparing him for the future.

He always remembered his father's advice, "Be like the water because no matter how many obstacles it faces, water always finds its way."

Understanding and Insight

Flexibility is a vital quality that enables us to adapt to life's changing circumstances and face challenges with grace. It acts as a source of mental stability and emotional resilience, helping us avoid breaking down in tough times and guiding us toward new opportunities and paths of progress. Let's explore the profound benefits of this essential quality.

1. We often see that things do not happen exactly as we want. Sometimes, our dreams, plans, and even relationships change. Flexibility enables us to harmonize with these changing situations.

When we are flexible, we can accept difficult situations and remain calm and stable. For instance, in a new workplace where the nature of work differs significantly from our initial expectations, flexibility enables us not only to accept it but also to work effectively.

2. There can be differences, disagreements, and conflicts in relationships. Flexibility helps us understand others' perspectives, fostering acceptance and empathy. It encourages us not only to put forth our viewpoint but also to listen to others and find a middle ground toward a "win-win" situation.

3. Flexibility strengthens our mental resilience, allowing us to stay calm and stable even in stressful situations. During such times, when others falter or give up, flexibility helps us maintain a positive outlook. For instance, when we are flexible, even after a project failure, we focus on learning our lessons rather than getting disheartened. We do not let stress overpower us; instead, we perceive it as a new challenge. We adopt a mindset that turns setbacks into opportunities for growth.

4. Those who are flexible are always open to change. When a new opportunity or challenge arises, they can take measured risks and explore new avenues. This not only promotes their personal growth but also lays the foundation for success in all areas of their lives. For instance, when faced with a financial or personal crisis, flexibility offers the strength and resilience to weather the storm and unlock new ways to create a better future.

In essence, flexibility means accepting the situation as it is, adapting to it by changing our behavior and perspective as needed, developing ourselves by learning something new from every challenge, and becoming a better version of ourselves.

Action plan:

Flexibility is a mindset you can nurture over time. Here are some ways to raise flexibility in your life:

1. **Reflecting on your situations:** Write down instances in your diary when your mind often becomes rigid and clings to a fixed idea or expectation, refusing to let go. Also, write what kind of flexibility can be helpful in that situation.

   For instance, you are watching a program on your TV and a family member changes the channel. But you take the remote control from them and switch back to continue watching your program. Now, you can pause, accept, and let them watch their channel for a while.

2. **Bringing flexibility to your thinking:** Remember that nothing in life is permanent. Sometimes, our plans do not work out. In such situations, when one plan fails, keep an alternative plan ready or be open to exploring a new one.

3. **Discovering new experiences:** Embrace new experiences in life. It could be learning a new language, taking up a new hobby, or trying out something new. This will enhance your adaptability.

4. **Practicing meditation and yoga:** Discover inner peace and harmony through the practice of meditation and yoga. With regular practice, you can gain better control over your thoughts and emotions, thus raising your flexibility.

   The practice of slow, deep breathing helps reduce stress and restore peace instantly. Hence, when faced with adversity, pause, take deep breaths, and consciously try controlling your reaction. This will help you develop the competence required to accept the situation effortlessly and unlock the most appropriate solution.

14

Boosting Your Energy Levels

As soon as the door creaked open, Raju called out to his wife, "Kajal, please, get me a glass of water. I'm completely exhausted today." As she handed him the glass of water, she asked softly with gentle concern, "Was it a tough day?" Raju sighed wearily. "Yes! This catering business is so labor-intensive. I don't know how Dad managed it. I lack the experience, and every event feels like a week-long battle just to satisfy everyone. Honestly, being on my feet all day tires me. If only I had worked with Dad right after college, maybe things wouldn't have been so difficult." His words trailed off in a whisper of regret as he slumped into his chair, exhaustion pulling him down. Kajal watched him drift off to sleep and quietly returned to her chores, lost in her thoughts.

The next day, the shrill ring of the phone broke the morning silence, waking Raju up. It was the supervisor's frantic voice, "Sir, there's a serious problem! There's no water in the hall today. The breakfast preparations have been stopped, and we still need to cook lunch. Time is running out, and I don't know what to do. Everyone is getting anxious here; please come quickly." Raju's heart raced as he replied, "Yes, yes, I'll be there in ten minutes," his anxiety mounting. He quickly got ready and reached the hall.

Chaos greeted him in the hall. Vegetables still hadn't been washed, and the dough hadn't been kneaded either. A few family members waited there anxiously. As soon as Raju arrived, he called for a water tanker, but it would take at least half an hour to get there.

Then a spark of hope flashed; Raju recalled seeing a tap behind the hall and rushed to check it, hoping to get some water. It was just a trickle, but enough to start work. The challenge now was to get the water inside. Hardware stores hadn't opened yet to buy long hoses. He instinctively turned to his staff and said, "Get some buckets. We'll carry the water in buckets inside and wash the vegetables at the tap itself." The staff were reluctant, as carrying heavy buckets of water seemed an arduous task.

Raju grabbed two buckets himself, took the lead, and walked toward the tap to collect and carry the water. He made two to three trips and managed to fill a tub. Inspired by his determination, his employees rallied behind him, their initial reluctance replaced by a shared sense of urgency. As they began collecting water, a few family members, their faces etched with worry, stepped in to help. Seeing their cooperation, Raju's enthusiasm doubled, and he carried on briskly with the task of collecting water while the cooks began preparing breakfast.

Raju, unaccustomed to physical labor and drenched in sweat, was completely exhausted. Although he had run out of energy, he pushed on and continued collecting water. His sheer willpower, innovative thinking, and hard work helped them overcome the crisis, and breakfast was ready just in time. By then, the water tanker arrived, saving the situation for lunch. Raju heaved a sigh of relief and, with a deep sense of satisfaction, sincerely thanked his staff.

This was Raju's first exhausting experience. He remembered his old self, how he would get angry at the slightest bit of exertion, how he would lounge on the bed after college, flipping through

TV channels, and calling out to his mother to bring him things. And today, he was a whirlwind of activity, working nonstop. He was amazed at the strength he discovered within himself. Where had this strength come from?

The main wedding event was scheduled for two days later, and around 400 guests were expected. Raju was fully prepared for the event and visited the bridegroom's house to confirm everything. When he reached there, the groom's father hurriedly approached him, saying, "Glad that you came. I was about to come and meet you." Raju hesitantly enquired, "Is everything alright?" The groom's father explained, "Yes, everything is fine, but my son's friends are insisting on a cocktail party. You'll need to manage the catering for that as well. Now, at the last minute, no other caterer is available, and the children are insisting on having this party. It can be hosted here, at home. But with only one day left, I'm unsure of how to manage it."

Raju pondered for a few moments and then confidently said, "Leave it to me, Sir. I will take care of it." Although he had committed, he was unsure how he would handle it. After returning, he called his staff and briefed them about the impromptu cocktail party. Since he had already agreed, they had no choice. Raju and his supervisor collaborated on the menu and compiled a list of items needed. They sourced the necessary items from a familiar shop that same night and made extensive preparations for the busy day ahead.

Early the next morning, Raju went to the market to buy fresh vegetables, fruits, and spices, then hurried to the venue to assist the cooks. By evening, thanks to everyone's tireless effort, all the arrangements for the event were in place.

Two days later, the wedding celebration concluded. Everyone praised the food, and some guests even promised to hire Raju for catering services at their future events. His staff also admired his intelligence and dedication. All their apprehensions about Raju's ability to run his father's established business were put to rest after he proved he could handle unexpected problems effectively and lead the team successfully to complete the work, even under pressure. Now, they felt confident about their future.

Raju was delighted to see everyone happy and surprised by his own competence in organizing a cocktail party on such short notice and smoothly managing both events. That night, when he got home, he felt very happy and content. He was not tired at all; instead, he began to play happily with his two-year-old son. His wife Kajal was also elated and felt as if everything had blossomed in their home.

Understanding and Insight

Nature has endowed all living beings, including humans, with abundant energy. But are we able to fully utilize our energy? Energy refers to our ability to work. When we work efficiently, we complete tasks on time, leading to positive changes in our lives, society, and the world. Conversely, due to a lack of ability to work, we may struggle despite having innate qualities, succumbing to fatigue. Therefore, we need to boost our energy levels and capability to work. If we are able to recognize and enhance our abilities and utilize them efficiently, we can witness wonders in our life.

Let's understand our inherent energy in detail, which can be categorized into three levels.

1. **The first-level energy** is what we use for our daily routine tasks, such as getting up, walking, speaking, cooking, performing office tasks, etc. As soon as this energy runs out, we start feeling tired and immediately declare, "I cannot work anymore now," or "I am very tired now." At the first sign of fatigue, we stop working. However, there is a big difference between feeling exhausted and actually being exhausted. By giving in to the self-imposed limits of our mind, we fail to access our second-level energy.

2. **The second-level energy** is used when we are physically or mentally tired but still need to work for a specific reason or situation. This energy is present in our body, but we only use it when necessary. For example, if there is a big event at home, a party, or a wedding, when students study all night before exams, or when someone goes on a picnic and climbs the highest mountains despite not being used to it. If this energy is utilized daily, our ability to work can also improve.
3. There is another type of energy called **the third-level energy**, which we usually cannot sense or feel. This energy is hidden deep within us and only surfaces in extreme situations when our body and mind are completely exhausted. For example, during a sudden accident, an unexpected calamity, a life-or-death crisis, or a natural disaster like a flood or an earthquake. In such situations, we push ourselves day and night to overcome the challenge. Then, this third-level energy gets activated, enabling us to accomplish seemingly impossible tasks.

Action plan:

1. Have you ever faced a situation where you worked beyond your expectations, pushing through fatigue to finish a task? Recall and write down such an incident. If you are not fully tapping into your energy levels, begin today and boost your capability.
2. To activate your second-level energy source, challenge yourself to work an extra 10 minutes each day, even when you are tired. For example, after finishing your office work, take on another task and start working on it. Similarly, after cooking, a housewife can spend some extra time organizing the kitchen. After studying, a student can dedicate more time to further study.
3. Whenever your mind says, "That's enough, I am too tired," while doing any routine task, push yourself for an extra ten minutes to

tap into your second-level energy reserve. Write down how you feel and what you think during those moments.

4. If you feel increasingly tired, close your eyes for some time and mentally command yourself to relax completely. Your energy will gradually begin to return. Take a few deep breaths and recall your goal. This is a simple yet effective way to beat mental and physical fatigue.

15

Wisdom and Intelligence

"Manjiri! Please listen to me," Aarav begged. But Manjiri was furious. "No, Aarav! There's nothing left to listen to or understand now. In life, all you can do is make excuses. It's your old habit. I've been watching you since our college days. At first, you said you wanted to be a mechanical engineer, then you decided to study computer science. You don't even know what you really want to do! You take on jobs with enthusiasm but leave them after a few months. And now, you have no job and no proper degree. How long can we carry on like this? I thought you would settle down after we got married, but nothing has changed."

Aarav tried to reassure Manjiri, "Trust me, I'll fix everything."

"We can trust someone who has a goal in life," Manjiri replied. "But you've treated life like a joke, and now life has made a joke out of you. I'm sorry, Aarav, but I think we need to part ways now." Saying this, Manjiri turned and walked away, leaving Aarav completely shattered.

A year had passed since that incident, yet Aarav remained trapped in despair, unable to move on and slowly sinking deeper into negativity. Troubled by his own thoughts, one day he made his way to the roof of his 30-story building, determined to end his life. As he reached the thirtieth floor by the elevator, he stepped out and headed toward the rooftop access. But just then, a voice echoed in the stillness, and he heard someone reciting a poem that made him pause:

Life is a gift; why give up, my dear?
Steady your mind through turbulent waves to reach the shore.
Let hardships be your love, a sword to pierce the gloom.
Celebrate struggles to bring forth your own light.
Resolve, and all you gain, the world is yours to claim.
Mend what is broken, fan destiny's flame.

Suddenly, Aarav stopped, turned around, and began walking in the direction of the voice. He knocked on the apartment door, and a man in his early thirties opened it. Living in the same building, he recognized Aarav by face but didn't know him well. With a smile, he asked, "Yes, what's it?" With a trembling voice, Aarav asked, "Who was reciting that poem?" Seeing Aarav's disheartened expression, the man invited him inside and introduced himself, "I'm Joy. You live here in this building, right?"

Joy was a talented computer programmer. He chose Robotics, the latest field in science, keeping the future in mind. He harbored a unique ambition to create a "Counseling Robot" that would listen to people's problems and help them through counseling. He was meticulously developing it with Artificial Intelligence (AI). Seeing Aarav's weary, troubled face, Joy immediately sensed that he was disappointed with life. Perhaps that was the reason he took an interest in Aarav.

Aarav spoke in a slow, despondent voice, "Yes, I'm Aarav. I live on the seventh floor; I was on my way to the terrace..." He then paused. After a tense silence, he gathered himself and said, "I was going there for some fresh air when I heard the poem."

Curious, Joy enquired, "Did the poem inspire you to come here?" Since Joy knew psychology, he quickly realized that Aarav might have been contemplating ending his life, and the poem had saved him.

Aarav nodded in agreement, and Joy, gesturing toward his robotic computer, said, "This is the poet whose poem brought you here." Aarav looked on in surprise.

Joy explained his purpose, "This is my robot, I've named it Bliss. I've been developing it for the past few years, designing it to understand emotional cues and offer personalized counseling through poetry and conversation. It's nearly ready now. I am scheduled to present it at the World AI University Conference, where leading inventors, juries, and global investors will be present."

Aarav, weighed down by negative thoughts, struggled to believe what Joy shared. He thought Joy was just boasting, trying to impress.

Joy sensed Aarav's skepticism and realized that he had lost faith in himself. He said, "Aarav, success in life doesn't depend solely on external achievements. Its foundation lies in our competence, and the basis of true competence is wisdom and intelligence."

Aarav gazed at Joy with a puzzled expression. Joy responded with a smile, "Intelligence is the power that imbues us with the competence to think, comprehend, and solve problems. It helps us discern between right and wrong. However, intelligence alone isn't enough. Wisdom is just as important. It teaches us how to analyze a situation accurately and act accordingly. Wisdom also helps us empathize with our own feelings and those of others, and to see things from their perspectives."

Aarav was listening half-heartedly and didn't fully understand the concept. Joy explained further, "Competence is the union of wisdom and intelligence. Merely having wisdom is not enough; the ability to apply it effectively is the true test of competence. Together, they empower us to confront life's challenges and help us achieve our goals."

Joy pointed at Bliss and said, "I've developed Bliss based on these two principles. It not only listens to what people say but also interprets their facial expressions and senses their emotions. Its inbuilt intelligence enables it to find solutions to problems, while wisdom gives it the insight to implement those solutions effectively. I was working on this when you came. How about a test on you? I know you're disappointed and frustrated. Perhaps Bliss can help you in some way."

Aarav looked perplexed and wondered, "Will this robot really help me? Will I be able to solve my problem and be free from it?" The old incidents flashed before his eyes once again.

"Hello, are you lost in your thoughts?" Joy asked. "Are you ready for the counseling?" "Hmmm," was all that Aarav responded, feeling the situation surreal.

"Look, you have to share your problems with Bliss for it to help you," Joy explained. "I designed Bliss based on a deep understanding of new ways of thinking and human psychology. Given how the human brain functions, Bliss has been programmed to support both left and right-brain functions. Additionally, I've added a new brain functionality called the 'Bright Brain.' The bright brain is programmed exclusively with positive things. It turns every negative word it hears into a positive one and responds accordingly, inspiring the person to think positively.

"For instance, if someone says, 'I'm troubled by my obesity and it's causing me several illnesses,' Bliss will respond, 'This problem of obesity has come so that you focus on your health, diet, regular exercise, and strengthen your body. Maintain a positive mindset and affirm, 'I am healthy,' recalling times when you were at your ideal weight and fit."

Gradually, Aarav's curiosity grew, momentarily setting aside his troubles. Eager to learn more, he asked, "Does this really work like that? How does the brain functionality you described operate?"

Seeing Aarav's willingness to understand, Joy said, "Yes, let Bliss explain everything further. It will first provide information to open up your intellect and then guide you with an action plan to put that knowledge into practice."

Joy activated the robot: "Bliss, start Aarav's counseling."

Bliss' blue eyes flickered slightly, and it spoke in its mechanical voice, "Aarav, let's first understand more about the brain. Consider a toy that laughs and jumps around when a battery is put in it and lies lifeless when it's removed. Similarly, our brain plays a vital role in our body and works the most. The human brain comprises a left brain and a right brain. The left brain holds past memories, and the right brain focuses on future thoughts. The 'Bright Brain,' located behind these, stores all the positive memories.

"We often rely on either the left or right brain, but we also need to develop the 'Bright Brain' within us, where our most beautiful, wonderful, uplifting, and delightful memories are stored. Tapping into this can help us overcome disappointment and hopelessness, enabling us to live life with renewed enthusiasm."

Aarav, intrigued, asked, "How is this possible?"

Bliss explained, "Aarav, our brain has become cluttered; all the memories of our life have taken over it. Our brain has carefully stored even those memories that are unnecessary. However, now we need to reprogram our brain by recalling life's satisfying and joyous moments and filling the 'Bright Brain' with these positive memories. Just like a baby shower where well-wishers bless the mother-to-be and the child to come with good health and happiness, similarly, we must reprogram our brain with happy, bright moments. We can then access these memories and stay happy and positive whenever we need."

Aarav's curiosity had peaked, and he asked, "Bliss, how will you help me in this entire process?"

Joy smiled, and Bliss replied, "I will remind you of the positive memories and achievements of your life—moments you have forgotten but that lie buried deep in your mind. These memories will help you realize that you are not just a collection of failures, but have also achieved many small successes in life. This exercise will inspire you to confront struggles with a positive perspective."

Aarav asked in surprise, "How? Is it possible that only memories can transform my life?"

This time, Joy interrupted, "Indeed, it does because our brain reflects what we feed it. If you feed it failures, it will create more disappointments. But if you nurture it with positivity and new hope, you will see a real transformation within yourself. Bliss acts as a counselor, and its most remarkable feature is that it uses your own words and feelings to reignite your motivation."

Aarav said doubtfully, "But I haven't achieved anything significant. There's nothing positive in my life."

Joy replied, "This very mindset is your biggest obstacle. Everyone has some accomplishments in life; you just need to recognize them. Let Bliss continue the exercise."

Bliss then began, "Aarav, let me hear what's on your mind. Can you recall a moment in your life that still makes you happy today, no matter how small it may be?"

Aarav was quiet at first, but then slowly replied, "Perhaps the day I topped my first project in college. Everyone praised me, and I felt like I could actually accomplish something."

Bliss quickly responded, "You didn't just top the project, but you also believed in yourself and impressed everyone with your work. That was the moment you recognized your true potential. Now think, if you could succeed in that project, why not in everything else? Doesn't it prove that there's something special in you?"

A gentle smile crossed Aarav's face as he realized he had overlooked many positive aspects of himself.

Bliss continued, "There must be many such small moments in your life that you may have forgotten, but these moments prove your competence. You simply need to believe in yourself again."

Aarav bowed his head thoughtfully. For the first time, he felt that maybe everything still wasn't over. A small flame flickered inside him, one he had ignored. He smiled and looked at Joy.

Joy said, "See, Aarav! Bliss helped you. It revealed your own strength to you. Now, you only need to understand that the challenges you face in life are simply the stepping stones on your journey ahead."

Aarav took a deep breath and said, "Maybe you're right. I should try again." Joy patted him on his back and said, "That's the right mindset. Remember, you're not a failure until you give up."

Aarav looked at Joy and Bliss with hopeful eyes. He knew the journey ahead wouldn't be easy, but he had found a direction; his new journey had just begun.

Understanding and Insight

Life is a series of events; just as shade is followed by sunshine, sorrow is followed by joy. But when one fails to realize this, they fall into the trap of getting caught up in every situation, succumbing to despair, and making decisions with a troubled mind.

In such situations, the power of wisdom and intelligence enables them to think, comprehend, and resolve issues. It helps them learn new things, understand the complex aspects of life, and make the right decisions.

In reality, the moment a problem arises in one's life, their "Happy Hat" slips off, and they stop feeling happy and start worrying. When they are unhappy, their thoughts also become negative because they are more receptive to negativity at that time. This shift in mindset hinders their ability to reach their goals, and whatever they want to achieve gets even farther away from them.

Therefore, no matter what happens, just as you make habits like brushing your teeth and bathing part of your daily routine to prepare for the day, you should also develop the habit of being happy, regardless of the circumstances. This will help you stay joyful in every situation life presents.

Action plan:

The human brain always stores rich memories. However, since both happy and sad memories are stored together, it can be unpredictable which one will surface at any given time. To ensure access only to positive, uplifting memories when needed, the brain needs to be actively programmed, much like a computer. Let's explore how to achieve this.

1. To begin, sit comfortably with your eyes closed for some time.
2. Gently place your hand on the left side of your head, over your left brain.
3. Then, recall a pleasant and joyful incident from your life.
4. When you feel happy, gently move your hand from the left side to the back of your head, where the "Bright Brain" is located, as if you are performing a refilling process. Just as you download an app onto your mobile, similarly, download the new positive

memory into the Bright Brain. This is also akin to copying a specific file on a computer and pasting it elsewhere for backup. Repeat this process with your brain.

5. After placing that memory in the Bright Brain, put your hand back on the left brain and recall another inspiring incident that evokes positive feelings. As you feel happy, move your hand back to the Bright Brain again.
6. Repeat this process with every happy incident.
7. Once all the incidents are transferred to the Bright Brain, gently tap it with your hands. This signals that your brain is filled with positive, happy emotions.
8. In the future, whenever you feel sorrow or encounter a sad incident, tap your Bright Brain so that the rich memories stored there will surface and help you stay happy even through tough times. This acts as a form of anchoring.
9. Slowly open your eyes with a positive mindset.

Happy incidents can range from the smallest to the most significant, such as your parents' loving touch, happily celebrated festivals, academic achievements, topping your class, receiving awards in school or college, moments of praise, or cherished gifts that brought you happiness.

Beginning with your childhood, recall every small and significant joyful moment in your life up to today. This will help eliminate the negativity within you and enhance your competence.

16

Transforming Others' Lives

Amit's life appeared calm and organized on the surface, but deep within, he constantly battled inner conflicts. He was the favorite teacher among his students at school. Everyone wanted to learn from him and delve into the depths of his thoughts. He was dedicated to his students' betterment, envisioning their bright future and committing himself to providing them with every possible support. However, after returning home, his energy and enthusiasm would quickly drain away.

His wife, Maya, harbored different aspirations. She longed for a life of luxury and comfort, wanting to be happy and well-off in every way. Although she married Amit under parental pressure, his modest income and simple lifestyle left her feeling disappointed and resentful. She imposed her desires on him, often mocked his earnings, and saw his simplicity as a barrier to fulfilling her fanciful dreams.

This made Amit feel disappointed and dejected. He thought, "I try to keep Maya happy all the time, hand over my entire salary to her, and bring her small gifts. Yet, she remains perpetually annoyed with me." Sometimes, lost in his mental turmoil, he would ponder, "Why shouldn't I just get away from this life, or end it altogether?"

One day, Maya crossed her limits. Jealous of her wealthy neighbor couple, she lashed out at Amit, sharply declaring, "Tomorrow, I'm going to my parents' house forever. You stay happy with your petty life here." Maya's words stung Amit deeply, and that night, with a heavy heart, he left home to seek solace on the banks of the nearby river. Tears streamed down his face, and his mind was burdened with endless questions. Throughout the night, he kept praying to God for help in finding his life's purpose, inner peace, and a way to overcome his sorrow.

He sat there all night, overwhelmed with confusion. As dawn broke, he noticed a few sages bathing in the river. After their ablutions, they began to leave. Amit decided to follow them, hoping they could show him a way to peace. By evening, they reached a village square, where their guru began his discourse. As Amit listened to the discourse, a wave of detachment swept over him. After the discourse, he approached the guru and said, "My marital life is full of turmoil and unrest, and I wish to renounce everything. Please guide me to inner peace and allow me to join your fold."

The guru, a wise and learned scholar, replied, "My son, it is natural to experience anger, malice, and guilt in worldly life. To find inner peace, you must overcome these and other negative tendencies of the mind. Even if you escape worldly life through renunciation, you cannot run away from these hidden tendencies within. They can surface in another form and cause suffering. Therefore, you must learn the art of living in this world yet remaining detached, like a lotus in murky water. Then, no harsh words or sorrowful incidents can affect your inner peace."

With folded hands, Amit said, "Revered One, I'm not as wise as you. I'm just an ordinary man. How can I rise above these tendencies? Please guide me." The guru replied, "You can attain the life you desire, but for that, you must learn to guide your thoughts in the right direction. You must focus on what you want, and not what you don't want. Further, it will greatly benefit you if you become a channel to give others what you seek from nature. It could be health, wealth, time, respect, love, knowledge, and so on. By doing so, nature and the laws of thought will certainly help you receive them manifold."

The guru further advised, "Start by making a list of at least eleven people, and become instrumental in bringing joy into their lives. Then watch how nature begins working in your favor in ways you have never imagined."

The guru's words deeply moved Amit, igniting a new spark within him. He promised the guru and returned home. From that day on, his perspective on life completely changed. He resolved to change not only his own life but also those around him.

One day, Rahul, a student in Amit's class, approached him with a problem. His family was struggling financially and couldn't afford his education. So, he had decided to drop out of school to support his family. Amit listened carefully as Rahul shared his dilemma openly and then said, "Rahul, every problem has a solution. A hardworking, talented, and promising student like you should never give up their studies. If you truly determine to move ahead, no difficulty can stop you."

He advised Rahul to tutor younger students and apply for government scholarships to meet his education expenses. Drawing from his own experience, Amit emphasized, "If you educate yourself, it will open doors to better opportunities for you in the future, ensuring prosperity for your family." He also assured

Rahul that he would stand by him for every possible support and continue to guide him.

Inspired by Amit's guidance, Rahul began tutoring, continued his studies, and eventually passed his exams with flying colors.

In the same village lived a widow named Geeta, who struggled to support her family. She had no steady source of income. Seeing her hardship, Amit was deeply moved and resolved to help her become financially independent.

He inquired about her skills and interests. She shared her passion for sewing and embroidery but didn't know how to monetize it into a source of income. Amit suggested she start by stitching children's clothes and gradually develop it into a business. He also recommended that she form a group with a few other women and try selling their products in the city.

Encouraged by Amit's support, Geeta gathered the courage to start a small tailoring setup at her home. Amit further contacted a city-based trader, who agreed to help sell her stitched clothes there. Through this collaboration, Geeta became self-reliant and, through her hard work, supported her family.

Now, Amit's purpose in life had changed. He began to nurture confidence, love, kindness, and peace in others' lives. He realized that true happiness lies in contributing to others' well-being, and by walking this path, he unlocked his inner strength. As he worked to bring positive change to others' lives, his own life blossomed with joy.

Understanding and Insight

Everyone has qualities that can uplift others' consciousness. Hence, to raise others' consciousness, embrace the qualities that elevate your own consciousness. Like the sun, become a beacon of light, inspiring others and illuminating their lives.

When you become instrumental in bringing positive changes in others' lives, transformation begins in your life too, elevating your consciousness.

Remember, you do not need to climb the mountain for others to admire and applaud, saying, "Look how high you've reached." Rather, climb higher so you can see others clearly from above. A genuine climb should stem from elevated consciousness, awareness, and consistent spiritual practice. You cannot be the source of inspiration for others without genuinely elevating your own consciousness.

Action plan:

There can be many ways to become instrumental in supporting and uplifting others. It does not necessarily mean doing something big or bringing about a significant change in their lives. Instead, even small gestures can inspire them, like appreciating someone, helping someone with their tasks to boost their confidence, sharing helpful information, providing enriching books to augment their knowledge, being a sincere well-wisher, or simply being present with positive feelings and thoughts, and so on.

1. First, make a list of eleven people you can help uplift.
2. Then change your perspective on them; otherwise, we tend to see everyone through the same lens of lowered awareness. We think, "They'll never change," "Nothing can help them." These preconceived notions cause us to treat them the same way. Instead, consciously focus on their positive qualities. Only then can you become truly instrumental in transforming their lives.
3. Express gratitude to them. Start by mentally thanking them and then say aloud, "Thank you for being in my life."

How will the importance and value of these eleven people on your list increase? The more you appreciate them through your positive words and gaze, the more their confidence will grow. While interacting with different people, your own qualities will also increase. Consequently, you will notice that your speech becomes free from criticism and your words become more potent. Even after these eleven people, you can continue to inspire and uplift many more.

17

Out-of-the-Box Thinking

When Amrit returned home from college, his mind was consumed with the idea of going on an adventurous trip. He told his father, "Dad, I have a 3-4 day break from college, and I really want us to go somewhere!" His father gently smiled and asked, "So, where do you wish to go?" Amrit smiled and said, "You tell me! Where should we go?"

His father thought for a while and asked, "So, you'll come along with me?" With a spark in his eyes, Amrit replied excitedly, "Anywhere with you is fun! I'll also get to hear your childhood stories." In a playful, mysterious tone, his father said, "Well then, get ready for a surprise trip! Pack your bag and mine for three days, and I'll take care of the rest of the arrangements. Do take some healthy snacks along; it will be fun to munch while we talk." Saying so, his father laughed, as he knew both liked to grab a bite intermittently.

The next morning, as the first rays of sunlight touched the horizon, they set out in their car. As they traveled, Amrit's curiosity grew. Eventually, he couldn't hold back and asked, "Dad, where are we going?" His father chuckled and, in a deep, soothing voice, said, "Wait for a while, you will get to know."

After a couple of hours of casual conversations, they pulled into a small village. Amrit's father stopped to ask for someone's whereabouts and then continued their journey. Amrit figured out they were heading to a village and wondered what was so special about that place that his father wasn't telling him. As he gazed into the open, he thought, "It must be something. Dad always thinks of something new. He is full of surprises."

It was Amrit's first experience of a village. He was captivated by the narrow, winding roads flanked by lush green fields on both sides and the fresh, clean air. He watched the farmers working in the fields, the small, simple houses, and children playing here and there; everything was new to him. Everything seemed wonderful, a stark contrast to the noisy, bustling city. Seeing the wonder in his eyes, his father smiled gently.

His father stopped the car in front of an old yet grand-looking mansion. From the outside, the mansion appeared simple, but when Amrit stepped inside, it was remarkable. The spacious hall was adorned with antique furniture and subtle modern comforts. "It feels like a royal palace!" he exclaimed, gazing at the stunning mansion with awe.

His father chuckled and said, "That's all the magic of out-of-the-box thinking."

Amrit didn't quite understand what his father meant. But as he looked around the room, his eyes widened. The room had a bed that hung like a swing, but the moment he sat on it, it gently settled down and rested on the floor.

As he opened the back door of the room, Amrit was in for a surprise; he felt like he was in a jungle. A simple outdoor bathroom was set up, surprisingly without a door, but a small shower was installed as if to offer the pleasure of bathing under a waterfall. "This is exactly how it was in our childhood days in the village," his father said, his voice soft with nostalgia. "We bathed under waterfalls or in the river. You wanted to know about my childhood—well, this is it."

By evening, they had explored the entire mansion. There was a treehouse-like platform to enjoy the feeling of being in a forest, winding wooden staircases, and a large wooden hall upstairs—everything reflected unconventional thinking. Very little cement had been used in its construction. The rustling of leaves and the soft fragrance of flowers brought a strange sense of peace.

After dinner, they relaxed on the swing-like bed. They were so exhausted that they didn't notice when they drifted into a deep sleep.

The next morning, the cheerful chirping of birds woke them up. Feeling refreshed, they had breakfast and set out to explore the village. As they walked along, they saw a horse trapped in a deep pit, and its owner was anxiously looking around for help. When Amrit's father approached him, the owner said, "If we fill the pit with soil, the horse will climb on its own."

Amrit looked at his father in surprise. The three of them began dumping soil into the pit. The horse slowly climbed out by pressing the soil down with its hooves, and after a while, it leaped out of the pit.

On their way back, Amrit's father smiled and said, "You saw, that's out-of-the-box thinking. We rescued the horse without hurting it." Amrit nodded and asked, "What is 'out-of-the-box thinking?'"

His father explained, "Out-of-the-box thinking means to think in a new and different way, from a fresh perspective. It's about perceiving, listening, thinking, and understanding incidents, problems, and situations from a different viewpoint. For instance, look at the mansion we are staying in; the architect who designed it thought so differently. They not only preserved the ancient heritage but also gave it new life with modern amenities. Similarly, when you can't find a solution to a problem, you must go beyond conventional thinking, beyond the old, set ideas, and approach it creatively, just like the example of the horse." Amrit started to grasp the topic, but it was not fully clear yet.

Later that afternoon, they visited a family for lunch. Amrit noticed that the head of the family had brought a watermelon. Both of his sons eagerly rushed to get it. The elder son said, "Dad, I'll cut it." The younger son objected, "No, you'll keep the bigger piece for yourself." The father also suspected that, out of greed, the older son might cut a larger share for himself and a smaller one for the younger one. With a clever twinkle in his eye, the father resolved the issue, thinking out-of-the-box. He said to his elder son, "You will have the right to cut the watermelon, but your younger brother will have the right to choose his piece first." The older son, realizing that he could no longer cut a bigger piece for himself, cut the watermelon perfectly in half.

Amrit witnessed another example of out-of-the-box thinking. He realized that if we develop the habit of out-of-the-box thinking, everyday trivial problems can be solved easily in creative ways.

After lunch, they returned to the mansion. After resting in the afternoon, they went out for a stroll in the evening. Amrit asked, "Dad, how can I develop this out-of-the-box thinking within myself?" His father replied, "There are several ways to do it. For example, you can pick a topic and think about it from all angles or try solving a puzzle to train your brain to think innovatively. Since we're talking about puzzles, let me give you one. You have to plant four saplings in such a way that they are all equidistant from each other. How will you do it?"

Amrit laughed, "Hey! That's very easy. Just plant them one behind the other with equal spacing. The problem is solved."

His father corrected him with a smile, "If they are planted one behind the other, the distance between the first and the fourth sapling will be greater than the others. But the puzzle is that all of them must be equidistant." "Oh! I didn't think about that," Amrit admitted, and began to think further.

After some deliberation, he said, "Yes, I got it. Plant them at the four corners to form a square." His father shook his head in disagreement and said, "If they are arranged in a square, the distance between the first and third, and the second and fourth will be larger. So, they won't be equidistant."

Amrit sat down, feeling a bit discouraged. His father encouraged him, saying, "This is an opportunity to think differently; try to think out-of-the-box. When you can't find the answer to a question, break free from conventional thinking and try a new approach. Ask all kinds of questions, discard anything based on old, preconceived ideas, and try to solve the problem differently. Otherwise, we tend to stick to the same thinking pattern and try solving issues with the same mindset. As a result, we feel mentally exhausted after some time. It is similar to the mental fatigue you are experiencing now."

Upon hearing this, Amrit stood up with renewed enthusiasm. He picked up four stones from nearby and, imagining them as the four saplings, began experimenting by arranging them in different ways on the ground. Suddenly, he had a breakthrough, a *Eureka* moment.

He realized that the solution to this puzzle was not two-dimensional but three-dimensional! The answer lay in forming a triangular pyramid with four vertices, each having a sapling planted at its corner. The key feature of this pyramid was that all its edges were of equal length, ensuring equal spacing between the trees.

He quickly arranged three stones on the ground to form a triangle, then placed the fourth stone on a mound of soil in the center. As a result, the four stones were evenly spaced.

His father was pleased with his unconventional thinking. He said, "Well done! Now you're truly able to think differently." Both returned to the hotel-like mansion, joyful and carefree.

On the third morning, as they got ready to leave for a temple located 40 kilometers from the village, they discovered that their car's tire was punctured. The hotel staff assured them they would arrange to get the car repaired and suggested they take a bus instead. Since it was only an hour-long journey, they agreed and set off by bus.

At one bus stop, Amrit noticed several people boarding the bus. Among them, two women got into an argument over a single seat. The first woman claimed, "I'll sit here because I came in first." The second woman countered, "I'll sit because I had already placed my handkerchief on the seat through the window." Neither was willing to give in, and the other passengers tried to make them understand. The conductor came and paused to consider how to settle the situation. After a few moments, he said, "Why are you arguing? Let the older one sit here." At that moment, the argument ended, and both women graciously offered the seat to an elderly lady with respect.

Onlookers on the bus couldn't help but laugh. Amrit saw how the conductor's out-of-the-box thinking solved the problem without any further conflict. He realized that approaching life's challenges from a fresh perspective is the best way to deal with them.

This three-day trip was not just a casual outing for Amrit but an opportunity to learn a valuable life lesson. He learned to perceive situations differently and, more importantly, understood that there could be multiple solutions to a problem. All it required was the right way of thinking. These three days were not only exciting for him but also a profound experience of learning and insight.

Understanding and Insight

All of us need to cultivate out-of-the-box thinking as it not only helps us solve our problems but also offers solutions to many global issues. Those who have the courage and competence to think differently can certainly find solutions to their problems. We face several minor problems in our daily lives. However, if we develop the habit of out-of-the-box thinking, we can address these daily challenges in novel and amazing ways.

For instance, sometimes, we may have so many tasks to complete in a day that they overwhelm us and hinder us from completing them as planned. In such situations, by thinking differently, we can accomplish more tasks more effectively and efficiently in less time.

Consider a woman who struggled to find time for prayer. So, she inscribed the prayer on her utensils so that she could recite it while washing them. Thus, she integrated her prayer into her daily routine while doing her chores.

Out-of-the-box thinking provides the right solutions. In this way of thinking, we connect with our heart through knowledge and meditation and discover several new solutions to a single problem. When our brain and heart work in alignment, our mind effectively synthesizes all the information and experiences we already have and utilizes them in innovative ways. This increases the likelihood of new ideas coming to our mind. Consequently, we can discover solutions to problems we might not have considered before. Thus, this thought process serves as a key to success across all domains of life, as it propels us to think innovatively and enhance our competence.

Action plan:

Out-of-the-box thinking is a skill that can be developed through consistent practice and an open mind. You, too, can cultivate this ability by applying the following strategies:

1. **Asking questions:** Whenever you face a problem, ask yourself various questions from different angles. This will encourage your brain to think more deeply and view situations from a fresh perspective.
2. **Breaking free from old, established beliefs:** For this, contemplate any old belief you hold. Contemplation involves understanding that belief in-depth and assessing whether it impedes or facilitates your growth and problem-solving abilities, and how. This process allows your brain to think more openly.
3. **Experimenting:** Do not be afraid of trying new experiments. While experimenting, you might make mistakes but learn from them and continue moving forward.
4. **Documenting ideas:** Make it a habit to write down every new idea. This is a thinking process in which you bring all your thoughts onto paper, allowing your mind to calm and empty, making room for more fresh ideas to emerge.

The purpose of these strategies is to exercise your brain. Every effort you make is an exercise. Regardless of the outcomes, consistently practice out-of-the-box thinking so you can develop the habit of always thinking afresh and innovatively, benefiting yourself, others, society, and the world at large.

18

A Pledge to a Delayed Response

As his confidence had grown by now, Aman decided to venture further into the jungle. Although he felt apprehensive and hesitant about the new challenges ahead, he moved forward.

It was already noon. The lush, green, vibrant, dense forest, alive with the melodious symphony of various animals and birds, offered an exhilarating experience.

Aman noticed some tall mountains just a short distance away. As he approached their base, an inscription on a rock caught his eye, which read: "Whoever crosses this mountain shall be deemed the victor." Aman contemplated whether he should take the risk to win.

Aman's company organized an outdoor team-building challenge to evaluate its employees' leadership skills, courage, resilience, and teamwork. This was not a typical outing; the company designed it in such a way that participants had to step out of their comfort zones and confront real life challenges.

Aman and his colleagues faced various difficulties and challenges in the forest; the main challenge was crossing the tall mountain deep inside the forest. The rules of the competition were clear: Whoever successfully crossed the mountain would not only earn the winner's title but also a major promotion in the company.

For Aman, the task was more than just crossing the forest or climbing the mountain; it was a golden opportunity to advance his career. He saw this challenge as crucial, both personally and professionally. So, he decided to overcome every hurdle and prove his competence.

Aman began examining the mountain and came across a small doorway bearing an inscription, "Solve the riddle to get the treasure, else perish!" He was excited after reading this and, ignoring what was written further, he stepped through the doorway.

The moment he entered, the doorway shut behind him, trapping him in a dark cave. He frantically tried to reopen it, but to no avail. Eventually, he gave up and sat down, exhausted.

He began to rebuke himself, "Why did I rush through the doorway? It would have been better if I had been patient, delayed my action, and thought carefully before deciding."

Now, his primary concern was time. Fortunately, the company had set no time limit and provided ample supplies, easing his immediate worries about his needs. He ate some food, drank water, and rested for some time, reflecting on his situation.

Just then, he recalled a conversation with his wife at a farmhouse. Back then, while trying to pluck guavas from a tree, he was unable to quite reach them. Therefore, he resorted to impulsively hurling stones at the guavas out of frustration, only to hurt himself. Observing this, his wife said, "Aman, stop. Anger will not help. Show some restraint. At such times, you need to pause for a while, think, and try again later."

Aman realized that in his fervor to succeed, he had acted impulsively. He should have delayed his response here.

A delayed response is given when one pauses for some time before reacting. It is common for people to react impulsively in certain situations and later regret it. For instance, if someone speaks abusive words to the other, they might retaliate in kind. This escalates the argument, and both eventually regret it. But at that moment, they do not realize that hasty and uncontrolled reactions only bring sorrow. They end up trapped in their own hasty words. Therefore, it is essential to learn the quality of delayed response. It teaches the art of pausing for a while amid incidents, thinking anew, and responding with awareness.

Recalling this, Aman calmly surveyed his surroundings. Just then, he noticed a beam of sunlight falling on the ground, a short distance away from where he was resting. He got up and walked toward the source of the beam, where he found another doorway with a small glass plate hanging on it. It had the words inscribed on it: "Why measure? Be the key yourself; recognize the signature of an illiterate and apply its impression."

Aman immediately realized that the door would open only by solving the riddle. He pondered over the puzzle, "There's no need to measure, and I'm the key to the door, but how? And I need to recognize the illiterate's signature—how do they sign? They give their thumb impression. So, if I'm right, I need to give my thumb impression on this glass plate, which is the key."

Aman quickly placed his thumb on the plate, and the door clicked open. He hurriedly stepped out into the open space outside. He breathed a sigh of relief and continued ascending the mountain from a nearby spot.

He had barely moved some distance when he stumbled upon another riddle written on a piece of paper, pinned to a tree. It read, "This ascent will be covered by the morning bell. Read this carefully and share your suggestion, as the above words will decide the winner."

As he read the riddle, a stream of thoughts began flowing through him. He was convinced that the solution to the puzzle was in the first line, "This ascent will be covered by the morning bell."

"Where will I find the bell?" he wondered and began searching. At a distance, he spotted a goat grazing with a bell tied around its neck. Filled with excitement and losing his self-control, he started chasing the goat.

After a long time, when he finally caught it, he began looking for more clues but found none, which left him disheartened.

"Aman, pause and give a delayed response, remain self-restrained," an inner voice urged, and he began reflecting on that quality.

If someone is fond of food, they tend to lose control at the sight of it. They need to learn to delay their response. When food is served, they should pause for a few moments and observe it mindfully. Eat only after practicing self-control. Otherwise, people become habituated to the instant gratification of their desires. For instance, if they see someone wearing their favorite color, they might feel an immediate urge to buy a similar dress and fulfill the desire right away.

In today's fast-paced world, everyone demands instant service. If they see something on their mobile, they instantly order, whether it is clothes, food, or anything else. The habit of delaying responses is gradually diminishing. This underscores the importance of cultivating self-restraint and delayed response in one's life.

Aman took a deep breath, regained self-control, and reconsidered the riddle, "The morning bell?" It could be either a school bell or a temple bell. But since there could be no schools in the forest, it must be a temple bell. The moment he got the answer, his face lit up with a smile, and he set off in search of the temple.

As he walked ahead, his eyes caught sight of a small temple atop the mountain. With night approaching and fatigue setting in, he gathered strength and reached the temple.

At the temple, he found a bell hanging with the next riddle affixed to it, which read: "This is the final riddle. Whoever solves it will reach their destination." It further read, "It has a head and a tail, but no feet. It has a belly and eyes, but no ears. But it runs without feet, as if death were chasing it."

As he read the last riddle, he sighed in relief. Ignoring his fatigue, he began pondering the riddle deeply. After prolonged thinking, he was convinced, "The answer is an animal. But which animal has no feet?"

"Perhaps an earthworm," he thought, but the notion of "fleeing as if chased by death" didn't quite fit. "Then what could it be? A snake?! Yes, that's the answer. The snake has a belly and eyes, but no ears, and, when in danger, it runs without feet as if death were chasing it. It's a snake." Aman grinned. He grabbed his torch and set out to find a snake's burrow.

As he searched, Aman began descending the other side of the mountain. At its base, he spotted a large rock with crevices in the surrounding ground. Suspecting it to be a snake's abode, he looked closer and saw a small snake burrow nearby. As he moved closer, he saw another sign—this time not a riddle, but an arrow pointing in a direction.

Following the arrow, Aman began to move forward; the dense forest began to thin out, and the path ahead gradually became clearer. After some time, he heard faint sounds coming through the trees. Initially faint, they grew louder as he listened attentively. He then realized these sounds were from his company's camp. His exhaustion turned into excitement as he quickened his pace toward it.

Soon, Aman reached the company camp, where some of his colleagues were already there, likely to have returned halfway. Everyone was astonished to see Aman, who had managed to cross the mountain alone.

Back at the camp, Aman realized that he had not only taken a significant step in his career but also learned the valuable lesson of self-restraint and the art of pausing and delaying a response.

Upon seeing Aman, the camp manager praised his hard work and determination. "You did it, Aman. You're the winner of this challenge, and you will receive a promotion too." Hearing the news of his promotion, everyone congratulated Aman, who smiled with a deep sense of accomplishment and satisfaction.

Understanding and Insight

One who is able to exercise self-control can alone achieve true success in life.

In fact, our subconscious mind is so deeply ingrained with past conditioning that we tend to react habitually, in the same manner we have done over the years, if we are not mindful. Without self-restraint, we react impulsively, driven by these ingrained mental patterns that are like maps etched in our brain. The moment an incident occurs, our mind quickly reacts, assumes, stamps, or concludes, believing it to be the truth.

For instance, the subconscious mind might say, "This pleasant fragrance is soothing, so bask in its experience," or "The weather is unpleasant today; I'm feeling lethargic," and so on. We immediately trust the mind, get caught up in its words, and start feeling that way. In this way, we accept the directives of our subconscious mind as the absolute truth and lead our lives mechanically, on autopilot.

To develop self-restraint and foster delayed responses, we must first break the old programming of our mind. For this, we need to respond differently to the incidents in our life. Only through these conscious new responses can we erase the deep-rooted patterns from our subconscious mind.

Let's understand it with another example. Imagine you were eagerly devouring your favorite dish, but a phone call interrupted you. After the call, when you returned to your meal, you realized you no longer craved it. This interruption made you aware of how much food you actually needed.

It shows that we most often mindlessly eat out of habit. The subconscious mind enjoys tasty food and impulsively declares, "Eat more of this!" This is called a reaction.

With this understanding, delay your responses in some situations, take a deliberate pause, and you might be surprised to notice that your decisions have begun to be right, whether they are related to health, relationships, work stress, or any other part of life.

In this way, train your subconscious mind to break free from this game of impulsive reactions with the wisdom of a delayed response.

Action plan:

With the pledge to a delayed response, learn the art of pausing before responding.

1. When you feel the urge to scratch, pause for a few moments and ask yourself, "How long can I refrain from scratching?" You may find that many impulses, like scratching or wiping sweat away, fade when you do not give them attention.
2. When anger arises, pause and observe its effect on your body. Observe where you feel a vibration in your body, notice the changes in your breathing, and the accelerated heart rate.
3. When you find yourself in an argument with someone, pause briefly and affirm to yourself, "I want love, joy, and peace, not arguments."
4. While meditating, resist the urge to instantly wipe away sweat or relieve discomfort in your arms or feet. Even after meditation, when you open your eyes, practice delaying your movements for at least a few seconds.

In this way, whenever you remember, consciously delay your responses with common sense and discernment to empower and enrich your life.

19

Loyalty at Work

Since childhood, Amol had been a big dreamer. While his friends played games, he meticulously sketched layouts of the company he hoped to build someday. He always aspired to create a significant venture on his own. However, as life often reveals, the journey to fulfill one's dreams is rarely straightforward and easy.

After completing his MBA, Amol decided it was time to start his own business. However, when he shared his plans with his family, they became worried. His mother expressed her concern, "Son, we don't have enough funds to help you start a large-scale business." His father, who was a salaried employee, considered the risks and challenges of running a business and advised Amol, "Listen, son, running a business is not easy. It requires experience and capital. Instead, a stable job is more secure."

Although Amol wanted to start his own business, he acknowledged his father's point that he should gain some work experience first. He thought it appropriate to speak to his uncle about this, as he was a well-established diamond merchant.

He immediately approached him for advice. His uncle, who highly regarded Amol, readily agreed to coach him. He said, "We are family. Join us, and you can learn a lot in this business. And we, too, need someone trustworthy like you."

Amol began his apprenticeship at his uncle's firm. He started learning the work with enthusiasm and dedication. He grasped every nuance of the diamond trade, including cutting, polishing, and grading. Gradually, his uncle's trust in him grew even stronger.

But one day, an incident happened that shook Amol's world. He was in the office storeroom when he overheard a hushed conversation between a craftsman and the manager. Their secretive behavior raised his suspicion. When he watched them closely, he saw them tampering with the diamonds. He thought, "This is a serious betrayal! I must inform Uncle immediately." But instead, he confronted the manager in anger, "What are you people doing? I'm going to report this to Uncle."

The manager was momentarily taken aback, but then he tried playing a trick. He explained, "Look, Amol, I've been doing this for years, and your uncle has never known it. You're new here; you don't yet understand how things work. If you stay quiet, I'll share the profits with you too."

Amol was initially stunned, but the lure of money persuaded him. He reasoned, "I just have to stay silent. I don't have to do anything wrong, and in exchange, I'll be well compensated. Besides, this will help me build my capital for my own venture! What's the harm?"

He failed to grasp the dangerous situation, a perilous swamp he was stepping into. For a few days, everything went smoothly according to the manager's plan. But, as the saying goes, no secret stays hidden forever; the truth always finds a way to surface.

One day, Amol's uncle noticed some discrepancies in the storeroom records and began investigating. It didn't take him long to uncover what was happening, and he caught the craftsman and manager red-handed. Furious, he shouted, "You've both betrayed me; I will hand you over to the police!"

The manager, perturbed, dragged Amol into the conspiracy. He said, "Sir, your own nephew, Amol, is also involved. He also received money in exchange for keeping quiet."

Hearing this, Amol's uncle was deeply shaken because he had always considered Amol very close and trustworthy. He immediately summoned Amol and asked, his voice trembling with disbelief, "Amol, what are they saying? Are you also a party to this?"

Amol could not meet his uncle's gaze. He hung his head in shame. As words failed him, his guilt spoke loudly in silence. He realized that he had committed a grave mistake, lured by greed. As his uncle's trust was shattered, the manager was fired for lacking honesty despite his competence. However, Amol was given a second chance.

"Amol," his uncle said, "I won't hand you over to the police because I know you didn't partake in this conspiracy. But you made a serious mistake by supporting them. If you are willing to work sincerely and rebuild the trust you have lost, I can forgive you."

Amol apologized for his mistake. His uncle then explained to him, "Honesty isn't just about appearing loyal to others. True honesty is when you hold yourself in high esteem by developing integrity. Your feelings, thoughts, words, writing, and actions should be in alignment."

All through that night, his uncle's words kept reverberating in Amol's mind, especially those about bringing integrity to *feelings, thoughts, speech, writing, and actions*. He wondered, "What does this have to do with honesty?" As he pondered, he picked up his diary and began to write.

As he wrote, he recollected the entire sequence of events—how he had dreamed of starting his own business, how his parents had disagreed. It was his uncle who believed in him and was prepared to coach him. But Amol had broken that trust for the sake of some money. Had he worked honestly, he could have mastered the skill and succeeded in his goal of starting his own business. Although he thought about his goal and even spoke about it openly, feelings of greed had taken control of him. As a result, his actions had deviated. In other words, his feelings, thoughts, speech, and actions were not in sync.

As he wrote all of this, he realized the importance of being honest with himself. He understood that he would become truly honest with himself only when his thoughts, feelings, speech, writing, and actions aligned. His greed had not only tarnished his honesty and competence but also damaged the trust his uncle had in him.

From that day, Amol firmly resolved to prioritize honesty and trust over everything else. Thereafter, he proved himself to be a diligent and loyal employee forever. A few years later, his uncle, a master at assessing the true value of diamonds, carefully assessed Amol's integrity. He eventually acknowledged Amol's competence and appointed him as the company's CEO, entrusting him with the entire business.

Amol finally reaped the rewards of his integrity. He took pride in his competence, having attained such great success, owing to his integrity and honesty. Thus, while sincerely working at his job, he reached this pinnacle of inner success, too, ultimately fulfilling his dream.

Understanding and Insight

Earning a livelihood is an integral part of our lives. Nature provides everyone with a specific field of work to earn their livelihood. In this pursuit, it is essential to uphold honesty, even when tempted by greed or driven by the fear of failure. Dishonesty inevitably comes to light someday, so we must protect the wealth of our competence and character through hard work, dedication, and honesty, allowing success to unfold naturally, enabling us to take pride in our achievements.

To achieve lasting success, it is essential to preserve the strength of our character, alongside our competence. Integrity is the foundation of character. When we do not think in line with what we say and we do not feel what we think, we disrupt our alignment, causing internal conflict. Such behavior may provide temporary relief, but eventually, in the long term, we lose. Therefore, before envisioning long-term success, we must strive to develop our integrity.

A strong character is essential in every facet of life. Staying committed and loyal helps build trust. Trust falters when actions and words contradict each other. Once the character is tarnished, restoring it is arduous. One has to pay a heavy price to correct one's mistake and regain lost trust. Therefore, whether at home or work, one must uphold one's integrity and honesty.

Consider this joke about three friends who were trying to one-up each other by exaggerating their fathers' extraordinary abilities. One said, "My father runs so fast that when he shoots an arrow at a target, he reaches the target and catches the arrow before it strikes." Not to be outdone, the second friend said, "That's nothing! When my father goes hunting and fires a bullet at a prey, he runs at such a speed that he reaches the prey and moves it aside before the bullet hits it." Now, it was the third friend's turn. With a mocking smile, he quipped, "Is that all? My father's office closes for the day at 5:00 p.m., but he is so fast that he reaches home by 4:30 p.m.!"

Well, that was just a joke, but it helps us introspect whether we are fully committed to our work or being dishonest. For instance, if an employee regularly leaves the office earlier than their scheduled time, or their feelings, thoughts, speech, and actions do not align, it indicates they lack integrity and honesty at work. Such people should stick to their time commitments, maintain integrity, and complete their tasks on time.

In this way, when you diligently work hard in every part of your life with dedication, honesty, integrity, and commitment, you pave the way for holistic development, enhancing your competence and leading you to the pinnacle of success.

Action plan:

1. In your journal, honestly reflect and write down: On a scale from 1 to 10 (with 1 being the lowest and 10 the highest), how honest and loyal are you to your livelihood goal as of today?
2. What temptations might push you to change your decisions, and why?
3. When faced with a challenging task, do you try to pass the buck on to others or strive to give your best and see it through?
4. How often does your mind procrastinate on livelihood tasks? What steps will you take to deal with this?
5. How committed are you in the various areas of your life—physical health, social relationships, financial responsibilities, mental maturity, and spiritual growth?

20

The Mantra to Tackle Incidents

One morning, as Rajesh stepped out of his house for his daily walk, a sweeper outside the gate inadvertently kicked up some dust that blew toward Rajesh. An initial surge of anger flared within him, and he scolded the sweeper. Even though it was clearly unintentional, the sweeper, displaying humility, promptly apologized and moved on. Despite the apology, Rajesh was still fuming, muttering to himself, "I don't know from where such people come; they have no sense at all, they've ruined all my clothes." Grumbling to himself, he walked ahead.

A little farther down the road, a cat suddenly darted across his path. Rajesh instinctively mumbled, "Oh! The cat also chose to cross my path this morning. As if the day wasn't bad enough already, this had to come my way. I wonder whose face I saw when I woke up this morning. Nothing's going to be right for me today."

But then, he abruptly paused and, remembering something, he said, "WoW! Queen Cat! I've been blessed to see you in the morning. Now that you have crossed my path, no one else will block my way today!" Saying that, he smiled and moved on, recalling his own words that made him laugh. While others might see the cat's crossing as a bad omen, Rajesh enthusiastically appreciated the incident.

Just a few days ago, while sitting idle, Rajesh was browsing YouTube when a video popped up with the title: "Say 'WoW' in every situation and move toward success." Intrigued, he clicked on the video and started watching.

The main message of the video was: Regardless of the incident, whether negative or positive, you should always say, "WoW." By saying this, the negative energy of the incident is turned into positive energy, and instead of harming you, it works in your favor. The results might not be immediately visible and could even seem negative at first, but with patience and faith, a positive outcome will unfold over time. To incorporate this into your life, begin with small experiments, and as your faith strengthens, apply it to bigger situations.

After watching the video, Rajesh began trying it out in some situations. Although he was skeptical, he thought, "There's no harm in trying it. Let me experiment with it in small situations."

Today was his second day trying this out. Sometimes, out of habit, he would get angry, but after realizing, he would say, "WoW."

After returning home and completing his daily chores, he reflected on his events for the day. As a cement contractor, his business hinged upon supplying cement to builders. A tender to secure a major cement quota was to open that day.

After reaching the office, he asked his manager to seek information about the tender. The results were out by the afternoon; the tender had been awarded to another supplier. When he learned this, he initially felt frustrated but managed to stay calm by saying,

"WoW!" His manager was perplexed to hear Rajesh say "WoW" despite such a significant loss. There was no sign of disappointment on Rajesh's face about losing the tender; instead, he was praising the outcome. The manager walked out, silent and confused.

That evening, the manager rushed into Rajesh's office, flustered and stammering as he spoke, "Sir, we have got the cement tender! They had just called to say that the previous supplier was unable to manage the entire order with full payment. Hence, we have been offered a 24-hour window to secure the cement against full payment with an additional discount!" Rajesh responded with a serene smile, simply saying, "WoW!"

As Rajesh started saying "WoW," it began to have a noticeable positive impact on him. Earlier, he would feel irritated by even trivial mistakes and would scold everyone in anger. But for the past few days, he had not scolded anyone. Even when, at times, he raised his voice out of habit, he responded with a "WoW."

After experiencing positive outcomes, Rajesh revisited the video more attentively to gain a deeper understanding.

The video explained a profound truth—Life presents us with countless incidents every day, and in every incident, the mind intervenes and labels them. Sometimes, it categorizes them as "good" and sometimes "bad." When things happen the way we want, the mind becomes happy and labels it as "pleasure"; when they do not, it starts feeling unhappy. In this way, the mind naturally divides everything, whether an incident or situation, into dualities, comparing them: good and bad, right and wrong, pleasure and pain, black and white, truth and falsehood.

However, when we say, "WoW," the mind gains understanding that no matter what the incident is, we should remain happy and accept it, regardless of its outcome, whether negative or positive. This eliminates our inner resistance and shifts our perspective on viewing incidents. When we start saying, "WoW," in every situation, we become capable of tackling them. As a result, the sorrow caused by negative events decreases, and we begin to see everything with a renewed, positive, and joyful outlook.

When we say "WoW" in any situation, our inner feeling changes, and with this shift, similar situations begin to get attracted into our life.

For example, a young person attended a job interview and was rejected. He was overwhelmed with negative emotions and began to think, "Oh! Every company is rejecting me. I'm not competent enough. What will happen now? I'll never find a job! I'll end up depending on others."

Now, even if God tried to offer him a job, he would not get it because of his negative feelings. If he were told to say "WoW" at that moment, would he agree? Of course not!

However, this is the truth. When one says, "WoW," their feeling turns positive. No negative thought can shake them and attract positive situations into their life. When they say, "WoW," all sorrows in their life diminish, and they become capable of living life with a fresh, optimistic outlook.

Rajesh also learned and practiced an exercise from the video: say "WoW" at the end of every sentence.

You cannot find a solution to your problem — WoW!

You struggle to master a skill — WoW!

You do not get your favorite food to eat — WoW!

Someone insults you — WoW!

Your business yields no profit — WoW!

All your tasks remain unfinished — WoW!

A loved one falls ill — WoW!

Your car makes a lot of noise — WoW!

You did not sleep well — WoW!

The exercise ended with a simple but profound instruction:

Take note of every such situation in life where you complain. Observe people, situations, and incidents that trigger resistance within you and consciously say, "WoW."

With this new understanding, Rajesh gradually developed the habit of saying, "WoW." He soon noticed that even those around him had begun saying "WoW."

Understanding and Insight

No matter how many ups and downs life presents, we should embrace every incident with an attitude of acceptance and surrender to the way life unfolds. Whatever the experience, say, "WoW," indicating that whatever is happening is for our good, and we have been given a new understanding and made capable of tackling challenges.

The moment an incident occurs, we immediately categorize it as good or bad, creating sorrow. With the understanding of "WoW," we can immediately overcome the resistance that arises from the incident. Besides this, it is a subtle way of showing our complete faith in the divine—that whatever happens, happens for the best.

Even if the current outcome is not what we desired, what is in the making for us in the unseen realm is the most appropriate and the best for us. God never intends any harm for anyone, but the way God works is far beyond human comprehension.

Therefore, whenever a negative thought or situation occurs, embrace it with an attitude of acceptance and say "WoW" so that it dissolves gracefully.

Action plan:

You can also cultivate the habit of saying "WoW" from today.

First, reflect and note down what kind of negative incidents happen most often to you during the day, or which events trigger the most negative thoughts.

Now, whenever these negative thoughts arise, you need to say, "WoW." Your mind may resist but still experiment with saying so.

After saying "WoW", wait for some time; do not expect immediate results. After some time, you will notice a shift in your energy, and solutions begin to emerge.

21

Emotional Competence

Arjun was just a child when he lost his parents in an accident. Since then, he was raised by his grandfather. As he grew older, the burden of responsibilities fell on him, and he became serious-natured even at a young age. He had only a handful of friends. Due to his serious nature or the responsibilities he bore, he learned to keep his emotions in check. While managing his responsibilities at home and outside, his true feelings were deeply suppressed.

Then, one day, his grandfather suddenly passed away. A few days later, while sorting through his grandfather's belongings, Arjun noticed an old box hidden under the bed. When he opened the box, amidst some old papers, he found a colorful mask. Its surface shimmered with vibrant hues and was adorned with strange, varied shapes resembling human facial expressions. He guessed that his grandfather, who might have performed in dramas during his time, had likely kept it as a souvenir from a stage play. Intrigued, Arjun took the mask to his room. Since night had already set in, he placed it on the table, planning to examine it more closely in the daylight the next day.

That night, when Arjun suddenly woke up, he saw the mask glowing. He dismissed it as a figment of his imagination and, turning to the other side, he drifted back to sleep. The next morning, when he woke up, the mask was just as he had left it on the table. After thinking for a while, to satisfy his curiosity, he picked it up and placed it on his face. As soon as he wore it, he could see everything, unusually bright and clear. However, when he tried to remove it, it seemed stuck to his face, molding itself to his features. It no longer looked like a mask, although Arjun knew he was wearing one. The mask had a special feature: after wearing it, he could see everything with greater clarity, but it also exaggerated his emotions.

Arjun got ready for work, and as he stepped outside, his driver greeted him with a smile. Arjun reciprocated, but as he did so, his smile widened more than he intended, and his face began to glow. Although his face appeared to radiate happiness externally, he did not feel that happy internally. He realized that his outward expression of joy was deceptive; the mask had exaggerated his joy, whereas he was experiencing an unsettling emptiness within.

Bewildered, he reached his office. During a meeting, when a disagreement arose and he tried to express his point to a colleague firmly, his anger turned into an unexpected outburst. His facial expression changed dramatically, and a hush fell over the meeting room; his colleagues quietly dispersed. Arjun couldn't understand how his anger had become so terrifying. He realized that the mask was pushing each of his emotions to their extremes, beyond his control, but he couldn't figure out how to break free from it.

That night, while Arjun sat alone in his room, a sudden power outage plunged everything into darkness. The mask immediately intensified his fear of the darkness. He began to feel as if shadows were emerging from the walls, and he screamed with fright. But as soon as he touched the mask, everything returned to normal.

This continued with Arjun over the next few days. When he felt hungry, he would overeat; his greed intensified. When he saw money, he worried it might be lost or insufficient. This started happening with nearly every emotion. He realized that the mask not only magnified his emotions but also took control of them. Still, he couldn't understand why all of this was happening.

Arjun was determined to uncover the truth behind the mask. This determination ignited a ray of hope within him. As dawn broke, he hurried back to his grandfather's room and, opening the box, began searching thoroughly. He soon found a diary with detailed notes about the mask. It explained that the mask intensified the emotions of whoever wore it to extreme levels. It also included instructions on how to remove the mask. As he read, a deep sense of calm settled over him.

The diary revealed, "This mask brings to light your suppressed emotions. When you accept all your emotions instead of avoiding them, learn to face them with patience and courage, and try understanding them, your emotional competence will begin to increase, and then the mask will come off on its own."

Arjun heaved a sigh of relief. The next morning, as he set out fully aware, he asked himself, "Am I truly feeling happy, or is this just fake happiness? What changes happen in my nature at that time?" Through honest self-introspection, he understood that his joy was not a pretense but a genuine feeling arising from deep within, from his core. He was genuinely happy and realized that real joy is found in the small moments of life.

Arjun then explored the root cause of his anger. Why did he become angry? What feelings surfaced at that moment? What desires, when blocked, triggered his anger? Gradually, he started observing the emotions that arose in his body when he was angry. He reflected on whether losing his temper was truly necessary. Was the anger that hurt him, increased his heartbeat, made him breathless, and stressed his entire body, really justified? Was it worth causing all this trouble over a small unfulfilled desire? Through deep, conscious reflection, he realized the utter futility of anger and learned how to overcome it.

Confronting fear was the toughest challenge Arjun faced. Whenever fear surfaced, he closed his eyes and faced his deepest worries in the darkness. He understood that fear was just another emotion, and by facing it, he could conquer it and become fearless. Once he embraced his fears, the mask started to loosen its hold on him.

As he accepted each of his emotions and faced them, the mask cracked and fell away. When the mask broke, something inside Arjun also shattered—his false identity. He realized his true self. It became clear to him that he had been wearing masks of seriousness and responsibility all along, while deep inside, he had always longed to live freely and fully, without any inhibitions.

Why was he doing this? In fact, when the sudden burden of responsibilities fell on him, he wore a mask of seriousness to handle the situation, but that was not his true nature. He had forgotten his true self by adopting various emotional masks and was afraid to face life's challenges.

He realized that accepting and experiencing every emotion was the key to understanding life. Incidents would continue to happen; they are part and parcel of life, but he needed to develop his competence and learn the art of observing and handling his emotions in any situation, rather than trying to escape them. That day, Arjun firmly resolved that no matter what challenges life presents, he would remain emotionally balanced and pursue what he truly wanted. At the same time, he would also discover his true self, his true being.

Understanding and Insight

Is being sorrowful, angry, or anxious our true nature? Or do we put on these different masks to hide our inner weaknesses?

Is living life with these masks the real life, or is there something more to do in life beyond them?

When such questions arise within, one begins to seek answers and embarks on a quest toward a new understanding. They realize that they often hide their emotions of fear, sorrow, and pain because they think, "What will others think about me?"

To avoid being judged by others, they resort to various emotions, like getting angry, pretending, or escaping them by spending hours watching TV or browsing the internet and social media. However, these actions merely suppress their sorrow rather than alleviating it, and they keep accumulating unnecessary resentment inside. Over time, this resentment either erupts like lava from a volcano or manifests as a serious ailment.

Actually, whenever we become angry, we should witness it deeply to understand its workings. This will help us unearth what is concealed within it. If we can confront what is being hidden, we can be liberated from these negative emotions sooner.

Whenever you speak to someone irritably or vice versa, negative energy begins to flow between the two of you. Both try to defend themselves by proving the other person wrong and themselves right, wearing the mask of irritation. With this, both succeed in hiding their weaknesses. At that time, they forget that being irritable and angry is not their true nature. If they act with wisdom and understanding, they can foster harmonious relationships with love.

From the story, we understand how incidents in life get ingrained in the depths of our subconscious mind. Even though the mind yearns to become empty, societal norms offer no such refuge. As a result, people find solace by putting on these emotional masks, and gradually, they mistake this temporary relief for the final destination and stop their journey there.

We will understand the final destination in the next chapter.

Action plan:

Each person constantly wears a mask of temporary emotions, forgetting their true, blissful nature. While navigating the ups and downs of daily life, they keep vacillating between extreme fluxes of joy and sorrow. However, with the clarity and understanding gained from this story, one can avoid getting stuck in these extremes.

For instance, if someone cannot control their anger, they need to use a technique to release it. This might include listening to cheerful songs or a motivational speech, watching a comedy film or show, recalling a happy event, repeating positive affirmations, practicing meditation, or engaging in a hobby. When they develop their Emotional Quotient (EQ), the competence to understand and manage their emotions, no emotion will be able to overpower them.

Now it is time to shed the masks of anger, fear, ego, jealousy, hatred, resentment, and sorrow. To do so, start observing yourself honestly from morning until night. Use the understanding gained in this chapter to reflect on the emotions, pains, and various thoughts that surface during your daily activities, what kinds of masks they are, and what you do under their influence.

22

Spiritual Competence

High up on a distant mountain, there stood a magnificent temple named the "Earth Temple." It was home to a revered Earth idol, where devotees would come to worship. Various traditional practices were followed in the temple, and people performed rituals in accordance with these customs, praying for the fulfillment of their desires.

Further up on this mountain, at its summit, was a massive "Sun Temple." The path to the Sun Temple passed through the Earth Temple. For those who visited the Earth Temple, the possibility of ascending to the Sun Temple was open.

There were primarily three types of people who visited the Earth Temple. The first kind would light camphor and then enter the temple. They would then fervently seek fulfillment of their desires. They lacked true devotion, but out of curiosity, they still ventured toward the Sun Temple. However, on their way, they encountered towering dark and white clouds and, upon crashing into them, they were injured and fell. Eventually, their mutilated bodies would also disappear into the abyss of nothingness.

The second kind of people would light camphor and worship in the Earth Temple. After some time, they would even close their eyes and meditate. However, due to a lack of self-discipline, they wouldn't sit still for long. They would soon get up and walk toward the Sun Temple. They encountered the massive dark and white clouds, too, and were injured on their way. Despite their wounds, they somehow managed to confront the clouds and reach the doorway to the Sun Temple. But in vain, they found the temple door locked. On inquiring, they learned that the key to open the door was a mantra that could only be obtained at the Earth Temple. They continued to knock at the door, wounded and exhausted, they finally collapsed at the doorway.

The third type of people would light camphor and sit in meditation with great devotion. They would remain absorbed in unwavering, focused meditation for a long time. When they opened their eyes, they would find a mantra inscribed on the idol. They would read and memorize it. While being in a meditative state, they would make their way through the clouds and reach the Sun Temple. Thereafter, with deep reverence, they would recite the mantra, and the temple door would swing open, allowing them to enter.

This analogy illuminates profound truths. The Earth Temple represents our life on Earth. We have come here to learn some vital lessons and gain such understanding that enables us to enter the Sun Temple. This is the true purpose of human birth, the true goal of our life.

But to enter the Sun Temple, we need to develop spiritual competence. In the previous chapters, we have understood the twelve qualities that help us cultivate the competence to succeed in various aspects of life. However, beyond these qualities, spiritual competence will guide us to our life's true goal, leading us to ultimate success. To attain this success, a strong foundation is essential.

In this journey, we confront the dark and white clouds that symbolize the dualities of life, like happiness and suffering, honor and dishonor, love and hate. Besides these, many temptations lure us; emotions such as hatred, jealousy, or resentment also arise within us. However, navigating these clouds, transcending these negative tendencies, we must train our mind to be steadfast, obedient, unshakable, and loving, to reach the Sun Temple, which is our ultimate purpose of life.

We have been bestowed a human body and mind that enable us to think and reflect, which distinguishes us from animals.

Saint Kabir has beautifully expressed this creation in one of his famous couplets, in which he compares the human body to a finely woven fabric. He says we come to this world wrapped in this fabric, our body.

The lines, *Jheeni jheeni beeni chadariya, jyon ki tyon dhar dini chadariya,* convey that God weaves this finely woven fabric of the human embodiment with great care. "Jheeni," meaning delicate, refers to the subtle intricacies of our physical body, and "beeni" means to weave.

Our outer gross body is visible, but within it lies the mind—invisible and far more subtle. While we readily cleanse the stains from our body, we often fail to even notice the stains of our mental patterns and tendencies.

As a newborn baby, when we receive this body and mind, they are pure and sacred. As a child, our mind is full of innocence and purity, free from emotions like hatred, resentment, and ill will. But as the child grows, our mind becomes contaminated with tendencies such as greed, lust, anger, pride, jealousy, and hatred.

Saint Kabir further elaborates that God weaves this intricate fabric with immense effort on the spinning wheel of eight chakras, a combination of the five elements—earth, water, fire, air, and ether and the three qualities—*Rajas* (hyperactivity and uncontrolled ambition), *Tamas* (inertia and indolence), and *Sattva* (balance and equanimity). But in ignorance, humans contaminate this sacred fabric with impurities. And when it is time to shed the physical body, they return this precious fabric to God, blemished by these stains.

When we borrow something ordinary, like a book or a car, from someone, we take utmost care to return it in the same condition we received it. Then consider this precious gift, our body—this finely woven fabric bestowed upon us, donning which we experience life on earth, learn our lessons, evolve, and ultimately reach the Sun Temple—the highest spiritual realm. How should we return this sacred garment, our body?

Saint Kabir urges us to don this fabric, our body, with such care that it remains untainted, free from patterns or tendencies—live a life that ensures this fabric is returned to God in its pristine purity, just as we received it, without any stains of tendencies or scars of sin.

Do you know why and when this fabric, your body-mind, becomes stained? What lessons are you meant to learn while inhabiting this body? And what exactly is the Sun Temple?

In fact, when you say that you have donned this fabric, this body, it means that you are not this body. You are not the fabric that you wear. Similarly, you have been bestowed with this mind and body; you are not them either. You are the formless, untouched living essence that people know as the Self, Lord, Allah, God. That is your true identity, and realizing it is true spirituality.

As children, we often live in this experience of our true essence, but as we grow older, we begin identifying ourselves with the body. We become attached to the body and the mind, believing it to be the "I," but the truth is that we have donned it.

Just as we need a life jacket for boating or 3-D glasses to watch a 3-D movie, we have been given this fabric of the human body on Earth, wearing which we can experience life on Earth. But we mistakenly identify this fabric as "I."

When someone else receives more than what we have, jealousy or hatred arises within us. When someone is praised, a pang of "I'm not praised" surfaces within. Or if our body is hurt, we say, "I am hurt." In this way, we sometimes identify ourselves with our body, at times with our mind, and sometimes with our intellect as "I," but this is not the truth. We perform tasks as if we were the body, mind, or intellect, which fuels the ego, leading to negative tendencies that stain the fabric of our body-mind.

Therefore, the profound truth is that so long as we live considering ourselves to be the body, this fabric will remain tainted. However, when we live life with detachment and function with awareness, knowing our true self, our true identity, and remembering that we are not the body, it will remain untainted.

Till now, out of ignorance, we have accumulated many stains, because we have mistakenly believed ourselves to be the body. Now, if we want to return this fabric untainted, we must not only cleanse these existing stains but also learn to wear this body-mind fabric with such care that no new stains are gathered. This is possible only when we are constantly aware that we have *worn* this fabric, and *are not* this fabric, not the human body-mind.

But who is this "I?" To unravel this truth, we need to turn inward to recognize our true self, seek our own identity, which is possible through meditation, through the profound inquiry: "Who am I?" Just as in the story, those who meditated in the Earth Temple could see the inscribed mantra on the idol, which opened the door to the Sun Temple; when we sit in silence, in meditation, the mantra, "Who am I?" will open the inner door to the Sun Temple, that is, the door to Self-realization, knowing our true self.

God has intricately woven this fabric for us; similarly, we must re-weave our fabric and rebuild our foundation, in such a way that we remember who we truly are, every moment. For this, we must gain true knowledge, know our true Self through meditation with closed eyes, ensuring this experience continues even after we open our eyes, always remembering who we truly are.

You have to acquire such inner competence that you remain steadfast even amidst life's challenges. So, tell yourself, "Whatever obstacles or tendencies arise, they are merely clouds. I must find a way through them." Do not let these clouds, the stains of your tendencies, jeopardize your faith, love, and joy. Move forward with understanding.

If you remain unshakable and aware, consistently chanting the mantra, inquiring, "Who am I?" you can effortlessly reach the Sun Temple—your true Self. If you begin to live by recognizing the real "I," the stains of the old emotional scars on the fabric will start dissolving on their own, and no new stains will be formed.

Best wishes to you for building such a foundation, for developing such spiritual competence!

APPENDICES

The Competence to Read the Book

Imagine a friend giving you a book, saying, "Read this book carefully, read every word attentively. Every word here is precious like a pearl of wisdom drawn from the depths of the ocean. If you truly understand their essence, your life will be transformed."

You do not give much importance to your friend's words at first, and occasionally flip through a page or two casually, only to set it aside. It is not that you dislike reading books; rather, they are a part of your daily life. You even read or re-read some books twice or thrice attentively, especially fiction novels, and enjoy narrating their plots to others.

A few days later, as you are sitting with your friend, another friend joins and expresses his gratitude to him, saying, "I can't thank you enough for the book you gave me. Reading it has boosted my confidence, changed my perspective toward life, and taught me how to live life in the true sense." Then, both of them concisely discuss the book's profound teachings. This piques your curiosity, urging you to read the book earnestly.

On returning home, you immediately open the book. As you read, you feel many closed doors in your mind opening, unfolding profound hidden connotations in the book before you. The next day, you sit down to read the book again, this time with complete concentration and awareness. Unknowingly, you begin to reflect on its content, grasping the book's essence and applying it in your life.

This imaginary story could become a reality if you commit to developing your competence in reading. Let's understand how you can do it.

1. **Read repeatedly:** Indeed, it is true that the first time you read a book, you rarely grasp its depth fully. But when you read it repeatedly, you gradually uncover the profound connotations in the book. This strengthens your memory, making it easier to recall key insights.
2. **Mark key insights:** To help recall, you can highlight or underline the key sentences with colored pens. When you revisit these marked sections, they get deeply etched in your mind, eventually influencing your life.
3. **Summarize the essence:** Write down the book's core message in your own words in your notebook so that, when required, you can read and implement it. This practice, like summarizing a film's storyline, hones your ability to identify and articulate essential messages. For example, after watching a movie, try to narrate its core story to a friend concisely. This will teach you the art of summarizing, helping you write the essence of the book as well.

By consistently following these three steps, you will be able to read books more meaningfully.

Now, you might wonder, "Which books should I read to develop my overall competence? Which qualities should I work on? And what essential capabilities must I develop to improve my life and walk the path of progress?"

A curated list outlining the minimum and maximum capabilities needed for a successful life, along with recommended books to help you improve your competence, is given below.

Sr. No	Minimum Competence	Recommended Book
1	Creativity	The Spirit of New
2	Communication	Mastering the Art of Communication
3	Concentration	Mastering the Art of Concentration
4	Decision making	Mastering the Art of Decision Making
5	Habit of Journaling and Contemplation	The Magic of Writing
6	Maintaining Relationships	Celebrating Relationships
7	Positive Thinking	The Source – Power of Happy Thoughts, Inner Magic
8	Self-Discipline	Coach Your Senses
9	Time Management	Mastering the Art of Time Management
10	Willpower	The Magic of Willpower
11	Work on Goals	Self Encounter

Sr. No	Maximum Competence	Recommended Book
1	Emotional Competence	Emotional Freedom Through Spiritual Wisdom
2	Health	The Source of Health
3	Spiritual Competence	Who am I, The Source of Silence, Secret of Awakening, Higher Answers for Truth Seekers, Journey to Enlightenment
5	Teamwork	Get Hired by God

You can mail your opinion or feedback on this book to:
books.feedback@tejgyan.org

About Sirshree

Sirshree's spiritual quest, which began during his childhood, led him on a journey through various schools of philosophy and meditation practices. He studied a wide range of literature on mind science and spirituality. After a long period of deep contemplation on the truth of life, his quest culminated in attaining the ultimate truth.

Sirshree espouses, "All spiritual paths that lead to the truth begin differently but culminate at the same point – Understanding. This understanding is complete in itself. Listening to this understanding is enough to attain the Truth." Over the last two decades, he has dedicated his life to raise mass consciousness.

Sirshree has delivered more than 4000 discourses that throw light on this understanding. He has designed a system for wisdom, which makes it accessible to all. This system has inspired people from all walks of life to progress on their journey of the Truth. Thousands of seekers join in a virtual prayer for World Peace and Global Healing daily at 9:09 am and 9:09 pm.

About Tej Gyan Foundation

Tej Gyan Foundation is a non-profit organization founded on the teachings of Sirshree. The Foundation disseminates Tejgyan – the wisdom that guides one from self-development to Self-realization, leading towards Self-stabilization.

The Foundation's system for imparting wisdom has been assessed by international quality auditors and accredited with the ISO 9001:2015 certification. This wisdom has been presented in a simple, systematic, and practically applicable form that makes it accessible to people from all walks of life, regardless of religion, caste, social strata, country, or belief system.

The Foundation has centers in more than 400 cities and towns across India and other countries. The mission of Tej Gyan Foundation is to create a highly evolved society by leading seekers from negative thoughts to positive thoughts and further, from positive thoughts to Happy thoughts. A 'Happy thought' is the auspicious thought of being free from all thoughts, leading to the state of supreme bliss beyond thoughts.

If you seek such wisdom that leads you beyond mere knowledge, dissolves all problems, frees you from all limiting beliefs, reveals the true nature of divinity, and establishes you in the ultimate truth, then it is time to discover Tejgyan; it is time to rise above the mundane knowledge of words and experience Tejgyan!

The MahaAasmani Magic of Awakening Retreat

Self-development to Self-realization towards Self-stabilization

Do you wish to experience unconditional happiness that is not dependent on any reason? Happiness that is permanent and only increases with time? Do you wish to experience love, peace, self-belief, harmony in relationships, prosperity, and true contentment? Do you wish to progress in all facets of your life, viz. physical, mental, social, financial, and spiritual?

If you seek answers to these questions and are thirsty for the ultimate truth, then you are welcome to participate in the MahaAasmani Magic of Awakening retreat organized by Tej Gyan Foundation. This is the Foundation's flagship retreat based on the teachings of Sirshree.

The purpose of this retreat

The purpose of this retreat is that every human being should:

- Discover the answer to "Who am I" and "Why am I?" through direct experience and be established in ultimate bliss.
- Learn the art of living in the present, free from the burden of the past and the anxiety of the future.
- Acquire practical tools to help quieten the chattering mind and dissolve problems.
- Discover missing links in the practices of Meditation (*Dhyana*), Action (*Karma*), Wisdom (*Gyana*), and Devotion (*Bhakti*).

Tej Gyan Foundation – Contact details

Registered Office:
Happy Thoughts Building, Vikrant Complex, Near Tapovan Mandir, Pimpri, Pune 411017, INDIA. Contact: +91 20-27411240, +91 20-27412576

MaNaN Ashram:
Survey No. 43, Sanas Nagar, Nandoshi Gaon, Kirkatwadi Phata, Off Sinhagad Road, Taluka Haveli, Pune district - 411024, INDIA. Contact: +91 992100 8060.

WORLD PEACE PRAYER

Divine Light of Love, Bliss, and Peace is Showering;
The Golden Light of Higher Consciousness is Rising;
All negativity on Earth is Dissolving;
Everyone is in Peace and Blissfully Shining;
O God, Gratitude for Everything!

Members of Tej Gyan Foundation have been offering this impersonal mass prayer for many years. Those who are happy can offer this prayer. Those feeling low or suffering from illness can receive healing with this prayer.

If you are feeling troubled or sick, please sit to receive the healing effect of this prayer. Visualize that the divine white healing light is being showered on earth through the prayers of thousands and is also reaching you, bringing you peace and good health. You can dwell in this feeling for some time and then offer your gratitude to those offering the prayer.

A Humble Appeal

More than a million peace lovers pray for World Peace and Global Healing every morning and evening at 9:09. Also, a prayer (in Hindi) to elevate consciousness is webcast every day on YouTube at 3:30 pm and 9:00 pm IST. Please participate in this noble endeavor.